STILLWATER COARSE FISHING

STILLWATER COARSE FISHING

MELVYN RUSS

THE CROWOOD PRESS

First published in 1985 by
THE CROWOOD PRESS
Ramsbury, Marlborough
Wiltshire SN8 2HE

Reprinted, 1985
Paperback edition, 1986
Reprinted, 1988

British Library Cataloguing in Publication Data

Russ, Melvyn
    Stillwater coarse fishing.
    1. Fishing–Great Britain
    I.   Title
    799.1'2   SH605

    ISBN   0-946284-96-2
           0-946284-83-0 (PB)

All photographs by John Holden, except on
pages 25, 27, 59 and 103 courtesy of Angler's Mail.

Typeset by Inforum Limited, Portsmouth
Printed in Great Britain at the University Printing House, Oxford

Contents

Introduction

Techniques in modern farming, industrial flash pollutions, abstraction by water authorities to supply drinking water to ever growing urban areas, treated effluent released from sewage works and even over-fishing have all contributed to an incredible burden on our one-time fabulous river fisheries.

In the nearly thirty years that I have been coarse fishing I have watched a frightening metamorphosis overtake our rivers. Waters that once yielded bumper nets of roach, chub and dace have been abused by man to such an extent that they are no longer worth fishing.

Natural banks have been piled in the name of land drainage, water supply and property protection, while the one-time vital seasonal flows are now history. To-day, when it rains, surface water hurtles seawards while during the summer months levels can only be described as a trickle.

Spawning sites have been ripped out by dredgers, regular weed cutting has deprived each season's new fry of a place to hide from predators, feed and grow to support existing stocks of fish. In consequence, whole year classes of some species have vanished from some waterways . . . but the picture isn't that black for the ever optimistic coarse angler.

Anglers in their thousands have realised that their future sport and enjoyment lies in man-made and natural stillwater fisheries . . . waters that can be managed by man, are relatively well protected from pollution and can even be regulated as to how many anglers fish them at one time.

Regular water levels, consistent water colour, prolific weed growth, scientific culling, easy biological analysis when there is trouble and thoughtful stocking or fish transfer have resulted in a stillwater fishing boom over the past two decades.

Big business has not been slow to rise to the challenge. Many large gravel companies that at one time capitalised on gravel extraction have now turned themselves into commercially viable fishery owners. For the companies it's good public relations. They feel that they are putting something back into the communities that they once disrupted by landscaping sites and opening up the redundant pits for water recreation, mainly angling and sailing.

Ready Mixed Concrete set the ball rolling some years ago with their highly popular Leisure Sport Angling Club, which has several dozen top class stillwater fisheries under its control. Redlands have also set up their own scheme. The Amey Roadstone Corporation, part of the massive Consolidated Gold Fields group, set up the Amey Angler's Association several years ago to manage all their worked out gravel pits, which number many hundreds throughout the country.

Stillwater fisheries of all types are here to stay and already their track record as top class big fish waters are a legend. The Tring reservoirs in Hertfordshire hold two records: the tench at 10lb 1¼oz and the catfish at 43lb 8oz. Redmire Pool – in fact it's a small lowland lake – has produced an official carp record of 44lb. A 50lb plus fish, which hasn't been accepted as an official record, has come from the same water.

Savay Lake, near Denham, Buckinghamshire, which is controlled by Redland, has yielded a breathtaking string of 30lb carp; while in Norfolk the Waveney Valley lakes complex is renowned for its mammoth carp catches.

Oxfordshire is the home of a string of massive stillwater fisheries. One particular gravel pit, the famous TC Pit near Oxford, has turned up so many big bream, including the current record, that anglers have stopped counting.

Down in Kent, Johnson's lake has built up a reputation of being the county's top tench water, and the pits at Sutton-at-Hone, in the same county, are prolific carp fisheries.

And so it goes on . . . with every county in the British Isles having its own stillwater fisheries whether it be gravel pit, lake, reservoir or pond. Some are known about and regularly fished. Others are fished under a veil of secrecy for fear of over exploitation or poaching. One thing is certain. Stillwater fisheries are the venues of the future . . . and we anglers must learn how to catch fish from them in a sporting and humane manner. That's what this book is all about!

1 Stillwater fisheries

A stillwater fishery can vary from a tiny farm pond, to a massive water supply reservoir or purpose dug gravel pit, or to a gigantic mountain lake moulded by nature many millions of years ago.

All have a special interest to the angler but before we attempt to fish any of them we must first fully understand their natural make-up, how they were formed, underwater terrain, life giving chemical levels and, where possible, fish types and populations.

PONDS

At the bottom of the fishery ladder comes the farm pond. Many anglers might not give this type of fishery a second glance, but they are always worth investigating because some of them do hold specimen fish.

Ponds have normally been around for many generations and are the home of tench, perch, roach and rudd. Because they are generally surrounded by trees and bushes they are organically rich and very fertile. Fishing a pond, however, can have its drawbacks. These small stillwaters often attract the attention of young anglers and in consequence they tend to get overfished. And they often contain many stunted fish.

Don't be put off trying your hand at fishing your local pond. I once fished a small Cambridgeshire pond that was no bigger than a bomb crater, yet it produced a surprisingly good bag of crucian carp and tench.

LAKES

Next on the list of possible fisheries comes lakes, which fall into three main categories; mountain lakes, lowland waters and finally ornamental man-made lakes.

Let's take mountain lakes first as they can present some very special problems to the angler. For the most part, these glacial or rift valley lakes can be dismissed by the prospective angler as worthwhile coarse fisheries. They do hold fish stocks like perch, pike and oddball species like powan and vendace which are of little sporting value to the angler. Their vastness and extreme depths can make pinpointing shoals or individual fish an almost insurmountable task.

Some of the more hardy pike anglers do plot the depths of some Scottish mountain lakes by rowing a boat around likely fish holding areas while taking depth readings with an echo sounder, but it is an awesome task.

Mountain lakes also tend to have high acid levels caused by the run-off of rainwater over granite type rocks, which eventually seeps into the lakes. This results in them being acid, infertile and holding sparse fish life other than the more hardy native brown trout.

Top of the list in the family of lakes are the highly fertile lowland waters, which are chemically rich and high in pH levels (alkaline) – ideal factors for supporting the vital food chain which fish like tench, carp, bream, roach and rudd – all fish we will be trying to catch – feed on. These include shrimps (gammarus), snails,

*Part of a 100lb bag of common carp caught in just a few hours by
Melvyn Russ and England international Bob Nudd.*

diatoms (algae), daphnia, larvae, blood-worms (chironomids), surface insects and tiny fish fry.

Lowland lakes are very often shallow, three to five feet being about the average, with very silty or clay-like bottoms caused by falling leaves which eventually sink to the bottom of the lake and rot. They also tend to have their shallowest waters around the edge, with a gradual deepening towards the middle. The banks are lined with trees and bushes while the margins are usually reed or bullrush fringed. These key fisheries hold almost every type of fish to be found in the British Isles, with tench, bream and roach being at the very top of the list. Rudd can be found in many waters, while there is always a reasonable head of pike to be had.

Ornamental lakes, like those designed and constructed in many stately homes and country estates by Capability Brown, also make very worthwhile fisheries. Those at Longleat House in Wiltshire are a prime example of a man-made coarse fishery. Here three lakes were formed in a descending chain by damming an existing stream and flooding the surrounding land. These lakes are at their shallowest, and often siltiest, where the stream enters; the deepest part is right at the foot of the dam wall.

THE NORFOLK BROADS

Technically, most of the Norfolk Broads are not stillwaters. The vast expanses of Heigham Sound, Hickling, Ormesby and Filby Broads are connected by dykes, channels and streams to rivers like the Bure and Thurne; yet for angling purposes they can be classed as stillwaters.

The Broads are man-made waters, although they may not appear as such at first glance. Nature has made an excellent job of camouflaging the centuries old man-made peat diggings by smothering the entire area with six foot high Norfolk reeds.

The Broads are one of the most celebrated pike fisheries in the British Isles, although fishing for certain types of species, notably bream and roach, has been on the decline over the past two decades. In general, the main Sounds can only be fished from a boat as the dense banks of reeds make it almost impossible for the angler to get anywhere near the water's edge.

Depths of water across the entire Broads system is fairly uniform, with five feet of gin clear water being the general rule. The bottom is for the most part a soft thick oozy peat and the main species from the angler's point of view, besides pike, are bream, roach, rudd with some tench and a few perch.

THE FENS

One type of water I class as stillwaters are the many miles of virtually unfished dykes which criss-cross the Cambridgeshire, Lincolnshire and Norfolk flatlands or Fens. Like the Broads they are interconnected to much larger rivers like the Great Ouse, Nene, Middle Level, Relief Channel and many more famous rivers. However, from June right through to October they are generally 'dead' waters, only being pumped to clear the waterlogged farm land when the winter rains arrive.

In my opinion, they are fabulous small stillwaters that hardly ever receive the attention of an angler except perhaps for the odd local angler in the 'know' and, of course, the inevitable school children.

The drains themselves vary in size from nothing more than a ditch you can jump across to a fairly substantial waterway four or five rod lengths wide.

Matured gravel pit with trees and bankside vegetation well established.

Because the dykes have been dug into rich black soil, the water they contain is often coloured. Depths can vary from just twelve inches in summer to five feet in winter – yet there is a wealth of fish like double figure pike, along with zander, big bream, roach, tench, some superb perch (which seem to have escaped the dreadful perch disease which ravaged the country some years ago) and even chub!

GRAVEL PITS

Along with the lowland lakes, the other important fishery from the stillwater fishing point of view must be gravel pits which dot the entire country. A massive house and road building programme following the last war meant a huge demand for sand and ballast, which had to be dug from the ground. This resulted in huge and sometimes ugly holes being left in the ground once the excavation had been completed. However, most of the sand, clay and chalk pits flooded leaving anglers with a string of first class fisheries, which have to be shared with other water users, sailing clubs and in some areas with naturalists.

Gravel, deep clay and chalk pits offer the angler some special challenges. To appreciate them we have to know how pits were dug in the first place. Many gravel companies use large cranes and grabs or buckets attached to draglines for removing the valuable sand. This means that below the water surface the gravel pit bottom can have what can be best described as a 'lunar' surface, for nowhere can a flat bottom be found – just a collection of potholes, undulations, small and large mounds, and an exaggerated corrugated effect.

An angler must understand these configurations before he even attempts to cast a bait, for fish will often show definite preferences where they will lie. There's little point in casting out a bait into six inches of water or an area that's devoid of fish because the terrain is unsuitable.

A newcomer to a gravel pit cannot expect to do well on his first outing unless he has been told where the fish are. A little exploratory work will have to be carried

out before serious fishing can start. With the aid of rod, line and plummet the angler should explore likely areas to determine the depths. A note should be made of all the readings taken over one small area so they can be studied at home.

Fish like roach, rudd and perch are not static and will roam all over the pit depending on weather conditions and food availability. However, pike remain fairly static at certain times of the year as do the bream and tench shoals. Carp are a little different and follow definite feeding routes which have to be located and plotted for later exploitation. So the first rule of

Normally covered by 6ft of water, this section of Ardleigh reservoir in Essex shows how varied the bottom can be. Hence the importance of plumbing the depths and seeking out fish-holding features.

gravel pit fishing is to get an overall underwater picture of what you are attempting to tackle.

It is only by using the plummet skilfully that the angler will be able to locate plateaus of fairly constant depth, shelves, holes and channels. These underwater variations were caused by the crane operator digging out a particularly rich vein of sand, and they are an important feature of gravel pit fishing. Gravel pits can prove to be heartbreak waters with specimen fish coming to the net one day, the very same swim refusing to give its riches the next.

On the whole, gravel pits are not the most scenic places to fish. The area might still be marred by mounds of spoil which nature tries to cover with coarse grass. Bankside vegetation is usually very scrubby, being made up mostly of hawthorn bushes, and often is completely barren. Some of the older pits are reed fringed, yet below the surface can look like a scrapyard. Very often when a pit comes to the end of its useful working life, the owners dump their old machinery into it. Old vehicles, sand cleaning machinery, scrap iron and even dumped cars litter the bottom. They attract fish life but can foul up an angler's tackle.

A word of warning. Gravel pits can be dangerous. Deep water can often be found right at your feet, so don't attempt wading to land a fish unless you can clearly see a firm bottom.

RESERVOIRS

Water supply reservoirs are probably the most exciting of all stillwater fisheries, and it's a shame that not more of them are open to the angler. Because of the superb water quality, abundance of food and lack of fishing pressure (angling tickets are normally restricted), fish grow to phenomenal proportions and include potential record breakers.

The King George group of reservoirs in Hertfordshire's Lea Valley hold mammoth pike, roach and rudd. Essex's famous Abberton reservoir near Colchester has turned up bream well over the British record during netting operations. Thirty-five pound plus pike, huge roach and eels have also hit the headlines. Cambridgeshire's Grafham Water is yet another man-made water that holds massive pike. The best on record approach 40lb, but catching them from the deep and featureless water can be difficult.

Reservoirs are generally built in much the same way as ornamental lakes, which means the deeper water can be found along the dam wall end, and the shallows border streams which keep the levels topped up.

2 Weather conditions

Stable water and air temperatures, it is said, invariably mean that fish will be relatively settled and probably in a feeding mood. Falling temperatures, and in particular see-saw conditions, will unsettle fish and catching them will be hit and miss. So picking the right time to fish a stillwater is critical.

But fishing isn't that clear cut. We can't always arrange a day off work when the weather is right. Our free weekends and holiday periods don't always fall in line with nature either. Most of us have to fish when we can, and make the most of it.

However, trying to understand what goes on under the water in certain types of weather can help us to put more fish on the bank. Some of the things that happen are obvious; others perhaps are a little more baffling. Some stillwater anglers won't fish a water unless the wind has been blowing steadily on one bank for at least three days. This stable wind direction, so they argue, pushes all the fish down to one end of the pit, lake or reservoir where they can easily be hooked.

Is it really that easy? Are fish slaves to this rule or are they free souls who follow their own instinct, which is usually to find food? From my experience the only fish that are affected to a certain degree by wind direction are trout and carp, who do travel down the wind lanes and mill about at the windward end of a water in the hope of picking up food. Other species don't really seem to care very much where they feed.

Anyway, is it really necessary to fish into the teeth of a gale during mid-winter,

with eyes streaming and teeth chattering, just to follow one particular theory? Why not pick a bank or promontory lying sideways to a breeze and cast out . . . you are still presenting a bait in the right area.

Wind has two effects on water. Firstly any sort of wind, even a light breeze, will cool the surface. This means that deeper lakes and reservoirs will have a band of water temperatures ranging from the coldest on the surface to the warmest at the bottom of the layers.

Therefore, the fish are likely to seek the more comfortable warmer waters at the greater depth. In warmer, more settled weather, exactly the reverse will take place: the deepest water will be coldest, because it's farthest away from the sun's heating rays; the surface layers will be warmest. This principle doesn't apply to shallower stillwater fisheries because the wind action tends to mix the various layers.

So water temperature is the key to catching fish . . . not always the way the wind is blowing. Fish will swim around a fishery to find a water temperature that suits them best and an area that can prove to be a productive larder.

I remember fishing a match on a large Kent lake which proved that wind direction has no bearing whatsoever on making big catches of fish, in this case bream. It was a cold, miserable but clear day at the back end of the season and the peg I drew had the wind blowing into my face. It wasn't a particularly pleasant way to fish and I remember taking thirteen bream for about 42lb on a mini open-end feeder. I thought I had the match sewn up. But on following the scalesman round, I came across a fellow angler who had been drawn almost opposite me on the other side of the lake and had fished a straightforward rig with the wind behind him. He beat me by a good 10lb, and when we compared notes we realised we had both taken good weights of fish from roughly the same distance and depth of water, which presumably must have been about the same temperature. The rest of the field had caught fish on the bomb, feeder and even float, but they hadn't reached anything like the weights we had taken. It's the sort of result that can knock the 'fishing into the wind' theory to pieces.

It would be very hard to pinpoint an exact temperature when fish will 'switch off' because it's too cold and come back on the feed when it's suitably warm. Every situation seems to be different. What applies to one species on one particular water doesn't necessarily apply to the very same fishery the next day!

What fish can't stand is rapid drops in temperature, and this applies particularly to stillwater fisheries. Pike and even carp will take a bait on the coldest of days, but a sudden cold snap can be a shock to their

Blown for 3–4 days by strong winds, even still waters can run as fast as a river.

Severe drought forces shoals of fish into deeper holes and channels. In severe cases, de-oxygenation kills thousands of fish.

system and no matter how hard you try to tempt them with a bait they will refuse to budge.

After a solid week of bitter cold conditions, the fish seem to adapt. They won't feed as vigorously as they would through the summer and autumn, but it will be possible to catch fish. However, rudd catches seem to fall right away and bream can prove to be very difficult.

At one time, carp anglers packed their gear away at the end of September, but these days it is quite usual to fish right through to March for the species. It is a lot harder going but by picking stable conditions, whatever they are, fish can be hooked.

Winter roaching is always productive and the fish seem to be in better shape throughout the colder months. Piking

traditionally gets into full swing during the depths of winter, and I have known anglers who have smashed through thick ice with a sledge hammer and caught fish, although for safety reasons it's not a practice I would recommend.

I have taken pike when the weather has been unbelievably cold. On one occasion my line was literally freezing to my rod rings and cat ice crept from the bank to the middle of the gravel pit – but the pike still moved to deadbaits. Falling temperatures didn't bother the fish, you see. The same thing had been happening every day for a week or so, and they had become used to the conditions and adapted themselves to cope.

If you want to take a series of water temperature readings to help you establish a stable period, then don't simply paddle

Though many species feed throughout the day, the best fishing often coincides with dawn and dusk.

The depths of winter still produce excellent fishing if you can discover where the fish congregate.

out into a lake and dip your thermometer into the water. That's of little use. Get yourself a thermometer designed with angling in mind. Mine is in a specially moulded plastic tube to protect it from knocks, and it has a ring attached to the top. Simply tie this to the end of your line and cast it out into the area you intend fishing. Try it at the furthest range and slowly work back to the bank. If you have a float attached you will be able to plumb the depth at the same time!

Finally, the wind's power can play some peculiar tricks on stillwater anglers. Have you ever fished a gravel pit and thought you were in fact fishing a river? The wind is blowing one way – but your float appears to be going in completely the opposite direction! This is caused by undertow and in effect is the surface layer of water being blown across a water until it hits the lee bank where the surface 'flow' sinks and doubles back in the opposite direction. Your float goes one way and the lower end of your terminal tackle, and more importantly the bait, goes the other. It's a problem common to stillwater fishing but can be overcome by choosing the right type of float and positioning your shot in the right place on the line.

3 Species

There are thirty-three species of fish on the official British Record (rod-caught) freshwater fish list – but just seven species interest the keen stillwater angler.

Carp, of which there are four varieties, tench and pike are probably the glamour fish of the specimen hunting world. Bream, roach and rudd have their followers, as do the more limited stocks of perch. Although all these fish are regularly hunted throughout the British Isles, very few anglers know much about their life-cycles, exact colouring (which can vary from water to water) environment, distribution and probably most important of all from the angling point of view, natural diet.

It's surprising how woefully poor is our own understanding of freshwater fish. A so-called record roach can easily be mistakenly identified by its captor. Actually, the fish is the result of a liaison between a roach and a bream or even roach and chub – a *hybrid* in other words.

Identifying true roach and rudd is always a hit or miss business for the layman. Even anglers who have fished all their lives can get caught out. There is only one correct scientific way of telling the two apart, and that's by removing and examining the pharyngeal (throat) teeth which vary in each species. However, I wouldn't recommend that an angler should ever kill a fish, especially to find out what family it comes from.

From the following information I hope you will be able to make an on the spot identification and then return the fish alive to the water. Does it really matter what a fish is: true roach, roach and rudd hybrid or a mix of roach and bream with a touch of chub?

CARP

Four of the main stillwater species – carp, bream, roach and rudd – belong to the cyprinid (carp) family so it would seem natural to start off by investigating the lifestyle of the true carp. However, the subject is a little more complex because there are no less than four varieties of carp, the grandest being the fully scaled common, followed by the striking mirror strain, the uglier, scaleless leather and, finally, the cheeky little crucian carp.

Carp are by far the biggest fish that live in lakes and gravel pits, although there may come the day when catfish outweigh them. The biggest fish caught in the British Isles on rod and line is a 52lb fully-scaled leviathan, but the official record still stands at 44lb. The species thrive in lowland lakes and waters that are very weedy. Redmire Pool and the equally famous Ashlea Pool in Gloucestershire are just two habitats in which they excel.

Carp are a shoal fish when they are young. Anglers can sometimes see a dozen

(Opposite) Suffolk specimen hunter Len Head with a near-30lb mirror carp.

or so fish up to double figures cruising around a water either enjoying the heat of the sun or on the hunt for food. When they become larger they tend to be more solitary.

Late May or early June sees the fish spawning, usually when the water temperature reaches the upper 60s Fahrenheit. Bull rushes, waterweed or any handy vegetation can be the chosen site for the eggs. Young carp put on flesh rapidly and can measure over five inches long after the first year of life. Their lifespan is probably harder to determine but it would not be unreasonable to assume that they would survive at least ten years depending on the angling pressure on the fishery they live in.

Carp are deep, thick-set fish and are easily distinguishable by four leathery barbels which hang in pairs each side of the fish's mouth scissors. Its face is rather extended with a seemingly small mouth positioned at the very end. The carp's mouth may look small but it can open up to quite a large cavity capable of swallowing fairly big baits.

The carp's caudal fin is large and paddle-like with nicely rounded edges. The anal fin is also rounded, but it's the carp's dorsal fin which creates the most interest. Its leading ray – it almost looks like a separate spine – is armed with a row of tiny teeth along the inside edge.

Scale covering of the common, mirror and leather carp varies greatly. On the common, the scales are very large and armour-like, covering the entire body. The larger scales are above the lateral line, reducing in size towards the fish's stomach.

The mirror carp is a very striking fish on the bank. Large parts of its body are completely devoid of scales. Just one or two areas usually have small clusters of large scales attached. Its relative, the leather carp, is usually scaleless and looks, as its name aptly suggests, to be made from leather.

The habitat often determines the colour tones of the fish, but basic colouring is much the same for each species. The common carp usually sports a splendid bronze golden coat of scales with a dark, almost black, ridge down its spine. On some waters this golden colour can be much lighter. The fish's flanks become lighter towards the lateral line and its stomach can be yellow at the lowest part. Mirror carp are a more variable dark and light brown mix. Some fish have been caught that almost look black. This type of colouring also applies to the leather.

The carp will feed on almost anything that comes within range of its food sensors (barbels). Food is normally rooted up from the bottom. Thus carp are predominantly bottom feeders, although many good carp catches have been made on surface baits.

Crucian carp are the black sheep of the carp family in that they don't really grow to any size. Whereas a 20lb plus common, leather or mirror carp would be classed as a good specimen, a crucian weighing over 3lb is exceptional. These relatively small fish are very easy to identify. They obviously look very 'carpy' but the give-away feature is its humped back, which sports a long dorsal fin, again armed with a serrated spine.

The species spawns around the same period as its cousins and a fish could reach just over two inches long in its first year of life. It is mainly a shoal fish that can live in waters hit by very low oxygen levels, which is why it is commonly caught from small silty lakes and overgrown ponds. These small coppery-bronze scaled fish, fully scaled and without barbels around the mouth, feed at all levels, taking bloodworm from the bottom, mid-water swimming creatures and food off the top.

Common carp, perhaps the most attractive member of the family.

TENCH

The tench is the one freshwater fish that anglers cannot fail to identify. Its body colour can vary from almost black, to dark brown and even a greeny-yellow, depending on the environment in which the fish is living, to a golden yellow along its stomach. The other giveaway pointers, other than the dark colour, are very tiny slimy scales (which make the fish tricky to handle at times), small bright red eyes and a short but deep dorsal fin with a rounded edge. Tench have small mouths, and like all fish that root around the bottom for food, sport a set of barbels, in this case one each side of the mouth. Although male tench are sleek bodied, the females can look extremely fat especially if the spawning season is late.

The species can be caught from rivers but it is noted mainly as a lover of stillwaters ranging from tiny ponds to massive water supply reservoirs. In early life they are shoal fish and it's not unusual for an angler to land several dozen from one shoal during a day's fishing. When the fish become older and slower growers, they tend to become loners. It's common to see single large fish cruising around just under the surface when conditions are ideal.

The fish is predominantly a bottom feeder, using its barbels and rubbery mouth to rummage over the bottom in the hunt for insect larvae and worms. It is rare for a tench to feed purposefully off the top.

PERCH

Perch are another species that can't be mistaken. Their bright livery of green scales across back and shoulders with almost milk white belly and distinct black bars running from backbone to well below its lateral line are a clear giveaway. If you fail to spot these markings (the black bars can be faint on some fish), there is always the spiteful looking spiked dorsal fin that easily identifies the species. This fin is made up of around fifteen wicked spines. The perch's fins are also bright red, very much like those of the rudd.

Perch are not lovers of open water and prefer the murky solitude of underwater snags, pilings, and branches to hide behind, hoping that some unsuspecting prey fish will come their way. These powerful fish are predators and feed ravenously on minnows, sticklebacks, their own kind, gudgeon, and small roach and rudd. They eat insects and shrimps but definitely show a preference for live fish baits.

Perch spawn is a marvellous thing to see. The female fish lays strings of bead-like eggs over underwater vegetation well before the fishing season opens in mid-June. The fry, which hatch after ten days, can often be seen by the thousand in the warm shallow water during mid-summer. However, their survival rate is low in that they can be eaten by their own kind during their first couple of years of life. The species also suffered a major set-back during the late sixties and early seventies when stocks nationwide were hit by disease which decimated whole fisheries, some of which have not survived the disaster. On other waters, which oddly enough seem to be commercial trout fisheries, they seem to be surviving and even increasing in numbers.

(Opposite) Tony Chester with his official record tench of 10lb 1¼oz.

Perch. Aggressive, colourful fish now making a come-back in stillwaters throughout Britain.

The perch is something of a mystery fish in that some stillwaters hold massive heads of stunted small fish, while other waters don't seem to hold any small fish at all, just the odd big fish. And when these larger and older fish die out they are not being replaced by new classes of fish.

PIKE

Pike are the other stillwater species that can't be mistaken, even by children. The long pipe-like body, flattened head, main fin clusters sited near the rear of the body and mottled green and white complexion mark it out clearly. Its main body colour is usually black or browny green along the backbone, various shades of green along its flanks – the exact tone can vary depending on diet and environment – with a yellowy or golden flecked stomach over white. The fish's flanks are camouflaged by a dappled effect which can be either irregular spots of greyish-white, or in the shape of streaks or bars. Each fish seems to have its own special attractive marking. The pike's head flattens out from the eyes to the snout and the bottom lip can extend

Melvyn Russ bags a 20 pounder – a milestone in any pike angler's career.

fractionally further than the top one. Two distinct lines of pore holes run from below the eyes towards the tip of the snout. Each fish is equipped with a fearsome mouth of razor sharp teeth which are set so that they point backwards towards the throat. The teeth around the edge of the mouth are larger than those set further inside.

The forward part of the pike's sleek body, which is covered in tiny scales, is almost devoid of fins other than a set of pectorals which are sited just below the gill cover plates. The main source of propulsion comes from a powerful caudal fin, while at the rear of the pike's back is a large dorsal fin and opposite that, to the rear of the stomach, is an almost equally large anal fin. These two fins boost the pike's swimming power.

Pike are flesh eaters, a point worth remembering when you're fishing for them. From early life they feed on any small fish that might cross their paths. These include bream, roach, rudd, eels, gudgeon, and small pike and trout, if they can get them.

The species, as a whole, is lazy and only feeds when it has to. Pike very rarely chase fish and often lie in wait for the food to come to them. However, they can move rapidly, using their powerful fins if they feel inclined to home in on a free swimming fish.

Pike are early spawners and it's quite usual for anglers to plot the late February and early March spawning sites where the large female fish can be caught. They are fully fit once the new season begins in mid-June.

BREAM

The common or bronze bream, is a fish that looks slightly out of proportion. It has a humped back, large slab-like body and tiny eyes and mouth which has no barbels. Body colour can vary slightly from water to water, but in general it is almost black along the backbone, through to a rich bronze-brown, lightening a touch towards the bottom of the stomach area.

Its dorsal fin is small in comparison to its large flattened body area, and the anal fin is long, being deeper along the leading edge. It has a reputation of being an extremely slimy bodied fish. Specimens around 3lb are common but bream above 6lb are considered trophy fish.

Bream love stillwaters and can often be seen patrolling the shallows through early summer. It's a shoal species and once one fish is hooked others usually follow. Feed rate slows towards the start of winter and may fade to nothing under extreme conditions.

Spawning takes place along reed beds with males and females crashing about in shallow water, often with their backs out of the water. Newly laid eggs adhere to vegetation. Growth rate varies considerably according to the location but a length of ten inches would be about average after four years.

The bream is a bottom feeding fish, eating nose down to pick up food such as bloodworm and insect larvae.

General body colour can be variable, although most fish are noted for their

(Opposite) A 6 pounder goes a long way to overcoming the bad reputation bream fishing has in some quarters. It, and bigger fish, is still worth pursuing despite the lack of a fight.

Typical stillwater roach. Big enough to be fun, and prolific enough to build into 50lb-plus bags for the competent fisherman.

lovely brassy golden flanks, dissipating by degrees to a white belly over a deep, fully scaled body.

Rudd and roach feed on much the same food. Shrimps and bloodworms, along with other crustaceans form the main bulk of the diet. Growth rates vary greatly depending on type of habitat, fish populations and food availability.

ROACH AND RUDD

To the casual angler, roach and the rudd can easily be mistaken as the same species of fish. However, there are subtle differences which can be spotted by careful examination.

Let's take a look at the more common roach first. The roach's mouth is small, and slants downwards at a very slight angle, marking it out as a mid-water and bottom feeder. Also, the start of the roach's dorsal fin is directly above the root of the pelvic or ventral fin, on the fish's stomach. The roach has a bright red eye, whereas the rudd has a more golden eye.

A roach's colouring can vary with habitat and age. Some fish, especially those caught from reservoirs, have almost black backs with silvery white flanks. Those caught from other waters look blue-black with brassy flanks and have tail and dorsal fins that are brown, and stomach fins (anal, pelvic and pectoral) with definite touches of orange or red mainly at the tips.

During April and May male roach develop white nodules around the head area. The female sheds her eggs on available vegetation, and the fry hatch around two weeks later.

Many stillwaters, large and small, hold massive heads of stunted fish, specimens that are all of the same year classes and size. This often happens because there are far too many fish in the water in relation to the food available.

When the fish are small they eat daphnia, when they become larger their diet consists of water snails, shrimps, waterboatmen, plus certain vegetation.

The rudd can easily be mistaken for a roach because of its similar size and colouring. However, a rudd, as previously explained, has a golden coloured eye, a dorsal fin which is positioned well to the rear of where the pelvic fin base begins, and has bright red fins (anal, pelvic and pectoral) along the stomach. Another pointer is the mouth, which is sharply angled downwards, marking it out as a mid-water and surface feeder. The fish has no barbels around the mouth area.

4 Tackle

To enjoy the best sporting opportunities, an angler must pick his tackle carefully, matching the power of the rod, ratio of reel and strength of line exactly to the fish that is to be hunted down. A look in any tackle shop window will leave the uninitiated angler bewildered and confused, for the massive range of fishing tackle manufactured in this country, on the Continent, the Far East and North America is overwhelming. Some of the tackle is poor quality, some is cheap but more than serviceable, while other brands are overpriced. However, knowing what's available, what job it has been designed to do and how much it costs will prove more than useful.

Always try to get expert advice before making any purchase. Tackle dealers can be helpful; many are anglers themselves and know what they are talking about. They should be able to explain in detail what a specific item of gear is, if you are unsure. Other anglers can also be a fountain of helpful information, but make sure the person you speak to knows what he is talking about. Specimen hunters and anglers specialising in catching one particular species are exactly in tune with tackle trends and will prove the most reliable guide to correct tackle choice.

One thing is for sure, an angler cannot expect to build up overnight a full range of tackle that will deal with all species. My tackle has taken many years to assemble and even now it's being changed from month to month and smaller items continually up-dated.

The final choice is made a little more complicated by your commitment to the sport. The angler who wishes to specialise in just one species – carp for example – would pay a high price for a specially designed and built carbon or boron rod. However, the angler can make a very worthwhile compromise at the outset by picking distinct families of rods, reels, lines and accessories that can double up to deal with fish of roughly the same power and weight. And it's for this reason that I have split this section on tackle into four clear groups. I believe that an angler can use a pair of carp rods to land pike; bream and tench tackle is very similar, especially if you're going for the bigger specimens. The same applies to roach and rudd, but perch gear is probably in a class of its own.

Before we take an in-depth look into tackle we must decide what types of waters we are going to fish and what size of fish are likely to be hooked. Even fish of the same species, but far different weight, require different power tackle to handle them.

RODS

A twelve foot carbon float rod is more than capable of landing smaller fish including carp to 10lb, bream to 7lb, large roach and rudd and tench to no more than 5lb. So here we have one tool that can do a whole range of jobs – but this rule doesn't apply when we get to the big fish league. I wouldn't dream of fishing a stillwater like Tring reservoir with the rod because I know the water holds 10lb plus tench that will either smash my outfit or leave me

Eventually, you will build up a selection of specialist rods for
float fishing, leger, and for specific species.

The nightmare of picking a new rod. Tackle dealer Chris Edwards and Melvyn Russ check over the latest carbonfibre match rods.

short of power to handle it. The same goes for carp over 10lb; and a rod of the type I have described is no match for a pike.

For some reason the choice of carp and pike rods has become something of a passion among some anglers. It seems that in certain circles it is better to have the 'right' rod sitting in a rod rest than actually to catch fish on it! My personal view is simple. My rods have to be long enough to control a fish properly, be powerful enough to cast heavyweight baits (when the need arises), give quick line pick-up on the strike and, finally, give me some 'feel' when playing a fish.

With Space Age technology finding its way into rod blank making we find that manufacturers are making thinner walled, smaller diameter rod blanks that in some ways resemble little more than fly rods.

Until the late 70s the main rod material was glass fibre. Since then we have entered a much more sophisticated world with anglers now fishing with carbon rods. Some carp anglers are even experimenting with boron: tungsten wire fused by boron gas which gives a rod a stiffish feeling and a smaller diameter. Even aramids like Kevlar are used in fishing rod production. These new materials have yet to be fully field tested, so our final choice is between carbon, which gives a rod lightness and a 'live' feeling, and glass fibre, which is slightly stiffer and heavier.

Rod blank makers have even been able to construct their rods in such a way that they flex differently under loading. There are two basic curves which a rod adopts when pulled at the tip a *compound taper* (sometimes known as a through-action) which means the rod starts bending just past the handle and then goes on flexing right through to the tip. The other action is called a *fast taper* with the rod arc starting around the midway section and then progressively bending more towards the tip. Some manufacturers take the science a step further by producing a *semi-fast taper* which is a compromise between the two.

RODS FOR CARP AND PIKE

One type of rod is usually suitable for piking and carping but the final selection is very much your own personal choice. A compound taper feels relatively soft through the mid-power range, finally locking-up at full power when under extreme pressure. In many ways it's a sporting rod to fish with, because as the fish fights back the angler can interpret its every movement. Carp anglers particularly like this action of rod for short range work.

Fast action rods are somewhat different and can feel like a poker. They are superb tools for casting large baits, like big pike deadbaits and 3oz carp leads, a long way. They are generally more powerful than compounds and can set a hook very easily at long range.

Final rod choice and fittings is yours – you are picking up the final bill. If you are very keen, then I would probably recommend a matched pair of either compound or semi-fast actioned carbons which will give you plenty of feel when a fish fights hard but lots of power at the top end of the range if a fish needs to be halted on a run.

Before you shell out a lot of cash (cheaper carbon rods cost around £50 with the more expensive around £90), it might be worth considering a pair of modern 'S' glass alternatives. You must remember that carp and pike fishing is generally a

waiting game and that the rods will spend over eighty per cent of their time sitting in rests, so glassfibre's extra weight is no hindrance.

The length of your rod is very important. Don't ever contemplate anything less than eleven feet long. That's the absolute minimum. A slightly longish rod is a very useful tool for controlling a powerful fish and distance casting, and some of the more forward thinking carp anglers are now using outfits thirteen feet long.

Test curve (tip power) is something of a mystery with manufacturers using a variety of formulae. Again, it's very much a matter of choice which power ratio you go for, but as a general guide anything bracketed between 1½lb TC and 2½lb TC would be perfectly acceptable.

Choice of rod rings is vital. The new generation of rings, with diamond hard inserts are virtually indestructable. Avoid any rod that's furnished with plain wire rings. They are relatively fragile, soft and tend to break easily at the welded or soldered joints. All my carp and pike rods are furnished with three legged one piece Fuji BNHG rings. They are not particularly light – the action of a rod can be killed off by over-ringing – but they are very robust.

Rod weight can be cut a few ounces by choosing the one legged Fuji BSPHG rings, which are more normally associated with fly outfits. However, Fuji do not dominate the ring market and it might be wise to take a close look at the range offered by Hopkins and Holloway who make the superb Seymo rings, and at the equally good and ultra-light Dynaflow rings made by Daiwa.

The number of rings on a rod must be right. Too many and the rod action is killed; too few and the line isn't correctly moulded around the curve of the rod when it's under full compression. The average fast taper pike/carp rod would carry eight intermediate rings plus a tip ring. A compound rod would probably need two more to control the run of line.

There is nothing worse than fishing with a rod that's got the wrong type of handle; you either don't like the feel of it, or it's fractionally too long and keeps catching you in the side of the chest when casting.

Let's take length first. I have four rods for piking and carping and they all have different length handles, but the one that feels the most comfortable for me has the centre of the reel seat positioned twenty-four inches from the butt. Rod handle

materials vary. I like natural cork because it gives me something warm (in winter) and firm to get hold of even when it's raining. The reel is held in place with traditional tough nylon reel seat rings. Rod handles can, however, be made up of rubber diamond cut handles or the recently introduced Orblon, which looks like a cross between high density foam and rubber. It makes excellent handles and will probably eclipse all other materials in a few years.

Reel seats can vary from simple rings, which can be infuriating as they often work loose, through to the zip-type Fuji

Fixed spool reels are by far the most popular, but a few highly experienced fishermen still prefer the old centre-pin design (left).

With reels, you get what you pay for. The very cheap Far Eastern models don't last a season. Top-quality reels will be going strong in 20 years time.

Reels are high-precision instruments. Keep them clean and dry in zippered pouches.

FS6SB snap lock reel holder, which can feel slightly uncomfortable to the more sophisticated Fuji FPS winch fitting made from carbon and stainless steel.

Carp and pike rods can be purchased from tackle shops fully built by the manufacturer, or custom built by your local dealer. Rods can also be built by the angler himself, thus ensuring that he gets exactly the type of rod he wants. *Rods and Rod Building* by Len Head, Crowood Press £6.95, is a useful manual for the home rod builder.

REELS

Reel choice isn't that difficult as there is only one criterion: it must be capable of holding between 150 and 200 yards of 10lb line. I personally use a pair of trusty Mitchell 300 fixed-spool reels for all my pike and carp fishing. This model is now being replaced by the equally robust 300 A range which retrieves twenty-two inches of line per rotation of handle. The Mitchell 410 A, even faster with a line pick-up of thirty inches of line per turn, is another good choice.

Many pike and carp anglers opt for ABU Cardinal 55s which have a skirted spool and mechanical bale arm trip. Other models that should be considered are from the Shakespeare Sigma Supra range, the Daiwa RG 1650 M or equal models from the D.A.M. and Ryobi stables.

For piking, and especially when fishing from a boat or spinning and plugging, a multiplier reel can be useful. Many of the small palm size reels are ideal, although the ABU Ambassadeur 5600C and 6500C with level-wind are probably the best known among pikers. For heavy duty fishing the 755 is recommended, as is the Daiwa Millionaire. The reel I use for this sort of specialist fishing is a Penn 930 Levelmatic.

LINES

There is a multitude of fishing lines on the market, but don't be fooled by the fancy names and packaging – many lines are made on exactly the same machines in Germany!

The main priorities in any line must be constant diameter throughout its entire length, plus a certain degree of stretch or give when pulled progressively harder; i.e. when a fish is fighting hard. Poor quality lines can be too elastic. They often stretch under the power of a long range strike. The worst lines are those that are brittle and won't stretch at all under a sustained pull. Lines like this part very easily.

In general, pike and carp lines don't have to be heavy duty unless you know you are fishing extremely snaggy waters. On an open venue 8lb to 10lb line should be acceptable. On fisheries with plenty of hang-ups and snags it might be better to fish with a line of around 15lb.

Monofilament by the mile. Pick a good quality brand to avoid losing a big fish.

I have listed the main lines on the market and I have picked ones that are in the 8lb breaking strain class, unless otherwise stated. It's worth checking the diameter of each make of line. Maxima, 0.25mm; Racine Tortue, (7½lb) 0.26mm; ABU Spinline (9lb) 0.28mm; Golden Marlin, 0.25mm; Sylcast, (7lb) 0.25mm.

Line colour seems to be important among some anglers. The dark brown Maxima is very popular, as is the Sorrel Sylcast. Many specimen hunters now favour black Sylcast lines. Line can be purchased in 100, 500, 600 metre (2oz jumbo) and 1,000 metre spools. The 2oz jumbo spools probably offer the best value.

HOOKS

It's very hard to spot the difference between a good and bad hook. An angler can easily see a poorly formed eye or blunt point; what he can't detect until a fish is on, is whether the high carbon steel has been tempered properly. Even hooks by the same manufacturer can vary from batch to batch. If you do find a good hook note the batch number and buy ample stocks to last you a couple of seasons. The outlay will be

Hooks by the thousand . . . there are so many makes and designs on sale that you can't keep up with it all. Most stillwater experts stick to the well-proven names and sizes.

Split shot in full range of sizes is necessary for complete tackle control. The best shot are smooth-edged and soft.

worth it!

Some of the tried and tested hooks for piking are made by Partridge, who produce a range of medium wire barbless trebles from size 4 through to 10. These hooks do have a barb on one leg, intended for holding the bait. From the same company comes the VB back to back pike hook, a size 8 single barbed hook brazed to a smaller size 12 hook designed to hold the bait. I am not very keen on the hook as I feel the wire diameter is too heavy.

Mustad also make a range of very nicely balanced trebles, from size 14 through to 1/0. Sizes 10 and 8 would be the normal choice.

Favourite carp hooks come from the Au Lion D'Or range, made by Cannelle of France. These hooks are needle sharp and very tough. Partridge offer the Jack Hilton carp hooks, plus a range of specialist hooks. Drennan Specimen hooks have built up something of a reputation for reliability. They are bronzed, have a barb which can be flattened with pliers, a flat eye and a reversed forged bend for extra strength. The Norwegian firm of Mustad also manufactures hooks suitable for carp fishing.

SPECIALIST TACKLE

For bream and tench fishing, there's a distinct choice of rods depending on the size of the fish you intend tackling. For big specimens, like bream over 7lb and tench over 5lb, plus in special cases very big roach and rudd, it would be best to choose an 11ft or 11ft 6in semi or fast taper carbon rod, with much the same ringing system as the pike and carp outfits. However, the rods shouldn't be anywhere near as powerful as the outfits mentioned earlier – that's if you want maximum sporting enjoyment. Rods that have plenty of 'tip feel', and have a test curve of no more than 1¼lb, should be ideal.

These medium power rods will be used mainly for fishing big stillwaters, like reservoirs and large lakes, where bigger specimens will be taken on long range leger and feeder outfits. The rods will be specially designed with distance casting in mind, and be more than capable of setting a hook in deep water and then playing a heavy fish to the bank.

Reels, in general, are much the same as those used for carp and pike fishing, although line strengths should be down-

Bait cans, mixing trays and livebait cans. All useful, and either shop-bought or homemade from old ice cream tubs and the like.

graded to 5lb or 6lb good quality monofil.

For dealing with smaller tench, bream and the mid-range and smaller roach and rudd, there is no better tool than the fast actioned carbon float rod mentioned earlier. A 12ft or 13ft rod can be the work horse in your rod armoury, being more than capable of dealing with tench caught just over rushes on bottom fished float tackle, or bream hooked on long-range waggler float gear.

Rod rings should be Fuji anodised match rings model No. BMRFG, or something very similar, but they must be strong and very light. Because the rod is fast actioned and bends well under extreme power, it should be more heavily rung towards the tip.

To match this rod I would select a much

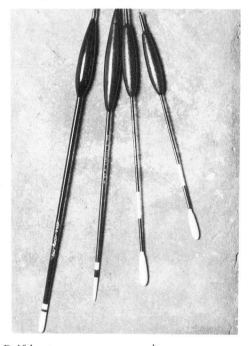

Driftbeaters, zoomers, wagglers, sticks, quills . . . there are thousands of different float patterns and sizes for stillwater fishing. To start, buy only those you really need.

lighter reel. I currently use a Daiwa 1300 XBM fixed-spool but any reel of similar size and ratio would do the job just as easily. Line shouldn't be any heavier than 5lb, and it will pay to have a couple of spare spools loaded with 4lb and 3lb lines.

The final outfit is for catching perch and the choice of rods can vary depending on how you want to catch them. I favour enticing them on small livebaits which means an 11 foot compound taper rod will be needed. The reel can be any medium size fixed-spool, loaded with 4lb or 5lb line. For those that want to take perch on spinners then a much lighter rod will be better. Most of the rods we have already mentioned are either overpowered or too long for this type of work, so something special will have to be chosen.

For spinning a 10ft carbon or glass rod capable of flicking out 1/8oz lures would be more than suitable. The Daiwa reel I mentioned earlier teamed with 4lb line, completes the outfit.

ACCESSORIES

So now we have the right rods, reels, lines and hooks for tackling our stillwater target

If you use a keepnet, make sure it is a really big one of soft mesh.

fish. All we have to do now is assemble the multitude of accessories and we are almost ready to catch our first fish. The list of extra bits and pieces you will need is almost endless. You will most certainly need a selection of small high quality swivels like the barrelled Berkley variety, and some 15lb cable laid Alasticum wire for making pike traces. For retaining and weighing big fish, a keepsack and a weigh-sling will be useful. Make sure they are legal in your water authority area. One of the most accurate scales on the market is the Avon Mark 7, which weighs fish up to 32lb in 1oz graduations.

A set of rod rests, either individual or on a bar system, will be required to hold your rods and bite indicators in place. Ideally, they should have threaded ends to accommodate electronic bite alarms like

Bobbins and many other bits and pieces are quite easy to make at home.

Neatly organised into compartment boxes and cases, tackle is much easier to look after.

Optonics and Herons which give a clear buzzing sound when disturbed by line passing over special sensors.

All small items of tackle like legers, shot, spare hooks and spools, forceps, bite indicators and a multitude of other items can be stored in redundant ice-cream tubs or even better, Tupperware containers.

For the really keen angler who will fish long sessions in all weathers, it will be worth investing in an umbrella, at least. Brolly camp, bed chair, special all weather gear – like a one piece suit and thermal Skee-tex boots – keep you warm and dry.

A high powered catapult will prove useful for firing out carp baits, while a pair of polarising glasses and binoculars are essential for fish spotting.

And, of course, you will need something

Rod rests are absolutely essential. Today's unit-construction outfits are most economical in the long run.

to retain your fish in. Buy the biggest keep-net you can afford. Personally I wouldn't use a net less than ten feet long, made of minnow mesh, and with a top ring of no less than eighteen inches diameter.

Finally, a rod carryall will be required to hold all those valuable carbon rods. Choose one of the nylon models that can hold up to half a dozen tubes which protect rings from knocks and bangs. Over the years I have used a multitude of boxes, baskets and shoulder bags to carry my tackle in – and none of them have been a real success. I have finally decided that a good quality rucksack, with external frame, is the real answer.

5 Knots

A knot is the last thing an angler wants in his fishing line, for every knot means a weak joint that could part at a critical moment. But it's a fact of life that we must use knots to join line to reel spool, hooks and swivels to bottoms and paternosters, feeders and shock leaders to main reel line. Every one of these attachments is a potential danger area even when the most careful precautions are taken. The most carefully prepared knot, tested over many seasons, can part for no apparent reason when subjected to a testing pull by a powerful fish. So it's vital to keep knots in terminal tackle to the absolute minimum and, where possible, to use alternatives like nylon stops and running beads. The ideal rig should have just one knot in its entire length, and that to join hook to reel line!

Before explaining the knots in most common use, let me say a few words about line care. There's little point in tying a 'pucka' knot if the line you're using is rotten. Being synthetic, nylon won't actually rot but it will chemically deteriorate if subjected to the sun's harmful ultra-violet rays and heat. An easy tell-tale test that a line is past its best is colour fade. A line will gradually change colour with age.

Even a freshly purchased spool of line could be past its best. And if you take your fishing seriously never buy 'special offers'. The line could have been lying on the tackle shop shelves for years and be a definite liability. Buy a well known line from a shop that has a lot of customers. Then you know it is reasonably fresh.

Never leave your reel and spools of line in direct sunlight. That's a surefire way of spoiling the whole batch. Keep lines out of the sun and heat and never leave a spool or reel in the back window of your car; that's fatal.

Many anglers fail to follow the simplest ground rules when setting up a rig. The most common fault is pulling tightly knotted dry nylon lines against each other. In extreme cases this can cut line strength to drastically low levels. All monofil fishing lines are manufactured under high tolerances from a petro-chemical by-product which melts when subjected to heat caused by friction. Line which has been subjected to this sort of treatment develops a series of tiny heat bubbles which can clearly be seen through a high powered microscope. The burnt area will be weaker than the rest of the line and easily parts under pressure. The simple answer to the problem is to wet the line with saliva before finally pulling any knot tight. The wetness minimises friction as the various turns of line tighten up on each other.

The family of knots in common use is extensive: Snell, Palomar, Blood or Clinch, Dropper, Uni-Knot, Bimini Twist and Water Knot being just a few. Each has its own specific job – although I feel that just a handful of well tried and trusted knots would suit most anglers' needs.

(Opposite) Knots are of paramount importance when you fish for big species on ultra-light tackle. Melvyn Russ lands a near double-figure carp on 1½lb line and size 20 hook.

Probably the most important knots are those used for attaching line to spade-end and eyed hooks. For tying flat eyed hooks I recommend the simple Blood Knot or the more intricate Palomar.

THE BLOOD KNOT

The Blood Knot is without a doubt the easiest knot of all to tie on hooks and all forms of links and swivels. Simply pass the end of the monofil through the eye of the hook or swivel, then take about half a dozen turns back on itself. Slip the end of the nylon back through the first loop formed by the eye and pull tight . . . after wetting the line!

This will form a tight spiral next to the eye and the spare tag of line can be snipped off, but make sure you don't cut it too short. The job is best done with a pair of stainless steel nail clippers.

THE PALOMAR

The Palomar is equally strong and the finished knot forms a tight ball of line around the eye when completed. Again, pass the line through the eye and double it

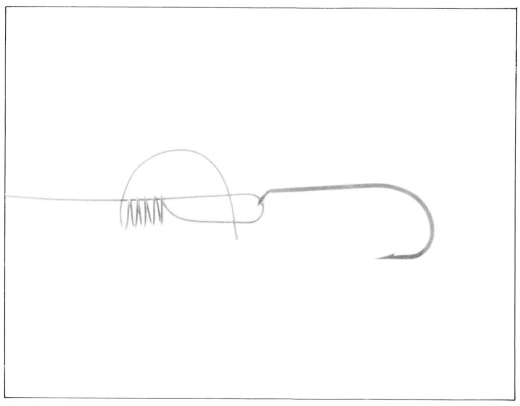

Blood knot.

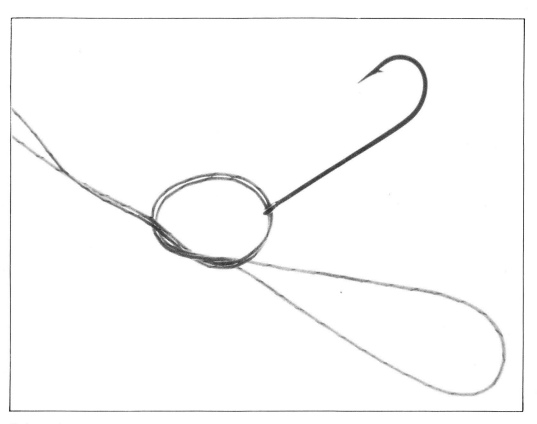

Palomar knot.

back for four inches. Letting the hook hang loose, tie an overhand knot in the doubled line to form a double loop. Try not to twist the line and don't pull it tight just yet.

Pull the trailing loop of line far enough so that it passes over the hook, or swivel, then pull at the spare end of line and main line at the same time until the whole knot gathers into a ball. Again, don't forget to wet the line before finally pulling home tight.

Of the two, the Blood is probably the most versatile and can be used for attaching bombs to paternosters, feeders to links, swivels to main lines and sliding leger beads to paternosters. It can also be made doubly secure, if required, by passing the tag end of line through the first loop and then back through the main loop of line before tightening.

THE UNI KNOT

For attaching hooks that have down turned eyes a different knot will have to be used, and for this job I would choose the uni-knot system which allows the hook to lie naturally along the line.

Thread the end of the monofil through the eye of the hook allowing for a six inch long tag. Hold the line against the shank to form a circle of line and then pass the free end back through the loop and round the shank as many times as required. Simply complete the knot by wetting, pulling tight, and trimming off the free spur.

SPADE END WHIPPING

For attaching spade end hooks I use a straightforward whipping knot. Take a loop of line, the length of tag depends on the size of the hook being tied.

Lay the loop along the shank with loop just jutting past the bend of the hook, and start whipping the free end of the line around the shank from the spade end backwards. After six to eight turns take the free tag and pass it through the small loop, wet and very gently pull tight. Trim off the spare tag and the knot is complete.

The knot can be a bit tricky on smaller hooks – I use it on size 18s but it is simple, neat and a proven knot. However, make sure the main line comes off the front of the shank. The line should never come off the back where it might be nicked by the out-turned spade. The same whipping sequence is ideal for making stop knots used for halting the run of sliding floats and beads.

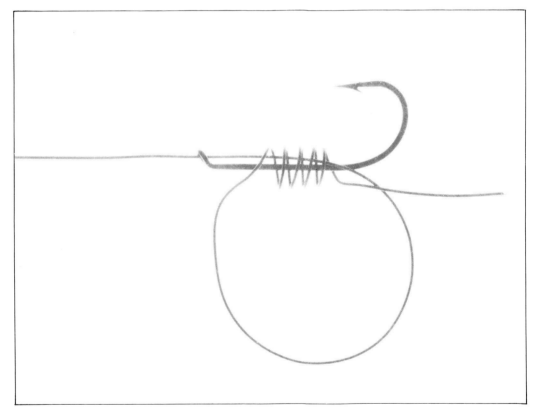

Uni knot.

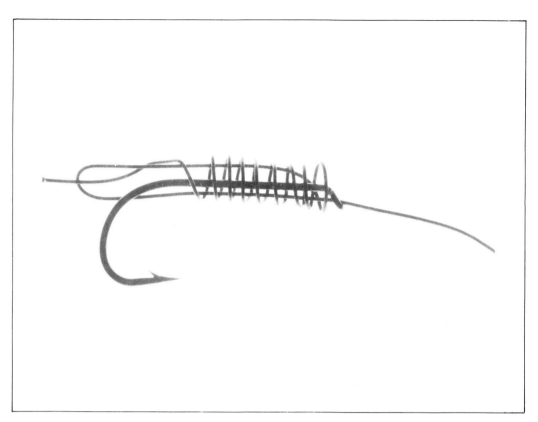

Whipping for eyed and spade-end hooks.

JOINING HEAVY
AND LIGHT LINES

Our final set of knots are used for attaching heavy and light lines to each other. Here we have a choice between the four turn Water Knot and the double headed Barrel Knot.

The Water Knot is the simpler of the two and this is tied by laying the heavier shock leader and main reel line parallel to each other with an overlap of about six inches. Take the two lines and tie them as one with a simple overhand knot, passing the entire leader length through the newly formed loop.

Repeat the sequence again by passing the entire leader line through the loop. Wet the line and pull both lines gently in opposite directions. This will form a ball type knot; be careful to trim the tag ends cleanly otherwise you could find the knot fouling the rod rings when casting.

The Barrel Knot is generally accepted by sea anglers as the safest and strongest leader knot of all. Take the main leader and form a simple loop. Pass the tag end through the loop a second time and gently pull both the free end and main line to form a small double eyed knot.

Pass the end of the lighter main reel line through both 'eyes' of the knot for about three inches and then pull very tight. Wet the knot and pull the main line for about another four inches. Next, wind the lighter line around the leader for about eight turns before doubling back the tag end which is passed back through the first loop formed behind the main knot.

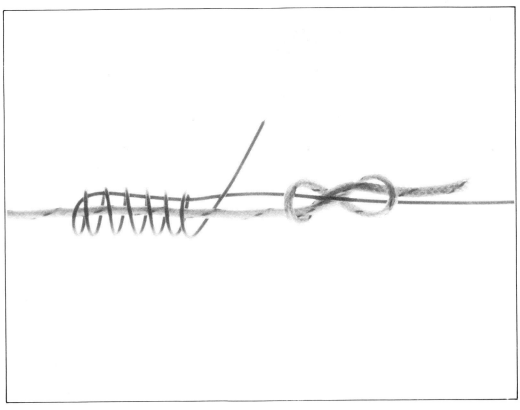

Barrel leader knot.

Wet the whole knot area with saliva and gently pull the main reel line and tag in one direction and the leader line in the other. The lighter line will snug down behind the knot and the ends can be trimmed free. I have tested this knot on a balance after joining an 8lb Sylcast line to a 17lb leader and it parted on a 9lb steady direct pull.

There are many other knots which are favoured by other anglers, but the few that I have explained should meet most needs. However, the rule should be to use as few as possible at all times, for every knot tied in a line means a weak joint . . . despite what some line manufacturers say about wet knot strength!

Hitting big fish at long-range is the ultimate test of knot strength and line quality.

6 The Law

The law is clear on angling: every angler must possess a licence to fish with a rod and line even if he is fishing on a private or club controlled fishery. Provisions for setting up the present rod licence system were set out by Parliament under the 1975 Salmon and Freshwater Fisheries Act, and the ten controlling Water Authorities in England and Wales interpret the letter of the law.

By-laws vary slightly from area to area, and they don't apply at all in Scotland where a different fishery system operates. In general, the law says you must have a rod licence *before* you commence fishing. Other laws are moulded to meet local requirements.

A day-ticket purchased from a club, tackle shop or on the bank is not a rod licence. It is a fee paid to the owner of the fishery for the right to catch fish from the water for the period covered by the ticket.

There are exceptions to the law. For example, in the Anglian Water Authority area children under the age of 12 are exempt, while youngsters above that age and up to 15 are entitled to a Regional Annual Concessionary ticket. Anglers reaching retirement age can also fish with the same licence.

But why have a rod licence system at all? That's the question that many anglers ask when they see fisheries polluted, rivers dredged and trees pollarded. Under the 1975 Act there is provision for a fisheries service, and this can only be paid for by one sector of the community – anglers. Water Authorities therefore collect monies through a rod licence system which is then used to fund a self-supporting fishery service.

The cash is spent on fish disease research, fish rearing, restocking, enforcement, and general fishery advice to clubs and sometimes commercial fish farms. Money is not generally siphoned off from the Water Authorities general account to pay for fishery work.

Usually one licence entitles the holder to fish with one rod. If you wish to fish with a second outfit then a further licence must be obtained. But study local rules carefully – in the Anglian WA area it is illegal to fish with more than two rods at any one time.

Many anglers get caught out by bailiffs, for not having the right licence. This particularly happens when there's an overlap of areas. An angler might live and generally fish in the Thames area but occasionally travel to the Southern WA area. He could be caught out for not having the right licence.

There are common rules which apply to most WA areas. One is the illegal movement of fish from one water to another. This particularly applies to pike anglers who fish with livebaits. An angler cannot, by law, catch livebaits from one venue say a river and move them many miles by road

(Opposite) Excellent fishing, particularly for the popular species like carp, is so cheap that it simply does not make sense to break the law. Fish of this quality can be caught for less than £2 a day.

to a stillwater for a day's piking. This rule is stringently enforced to combat the possible spread of disease.

Once an angler has purchased the correct licence for the region he intends fishing in, he can use a rod and line to catch coarse fish from June 16 through to March 14. The only authority where this does not apply is the South-West WA which covers Devon and Cornwall. Here, there is no close-season. In parts of Lincolnshire it is possible to fish enclosed stillwaters all year; while in Yorkshire the season starts and closes two weeks earlier than elsewhere in the country.

Bailiffs should carry a warrant card. They have the same powers as a police constable, giving them the right of entry to private land and powers to request information from anglers who cannot produce a current rod licence. A bailiff can also inspect fishing equipment, like keepnets, to check that they are long enough and that mesh sizes meet local regulations.

An angler who cannot produce a licence will be given an Offence Report by the bailiff. The angler then has seven days to produce a current licence at his nearest authority office. Failure to supply a

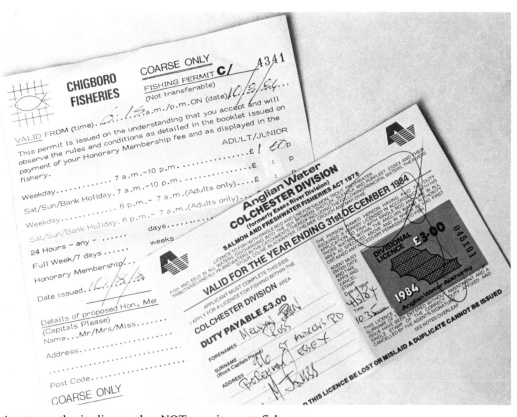

A water authority licence does NOT permit you to fish every water within its jurisdiction. You also must have the necessary day permit or club card.

Melvyn Russ and England team member Bob Nudd with carp hooked on long-range float tackle.

Doug Wood and a big mirror carp hooked on Opening Day.

Not a monster by any means, but great sport even so. John Watson with a 10lb fish hooked from the Norfolk Broads.

*Eels are not everyone's cup of tea. Terry Jefferson specialises
in them – and this 5lb 6oz fish is his biggest to date.*

licence in the given time usually results in the offender being summoned.

Anglers generally do not appear in court. Most plead guilty by letter and are fined £10, plus £10 costs. If a bailiff finds he has been given a false name and address but still manages to track down the offender, a hefty fine is usually imposed.

CAUTION
A rod licence doesn't give an angler the right to fish. Most fisheries are private, being either controlled by a commercial business, associations and clubs or private owners.

Entry to commercial or club controlled fisheries is easy. Buy a season or day ticket, or join the club. When fishing is in the hands of a private owner, a direct approach will have to be made to inquire if fishing is possible.

In general, landowners aren't against anglers unless some previous thoughtless fisherman has left a gate open which has allowed valuable cattle to stray. Farmers get irate if anglers drop litter, in particular polythene bags which get eaten by cattle. So, when you have finished your day's sport clear up your swim. Don't leave unsightly rubbish strewn on the bank. Take home all your unwanted line and hooks.

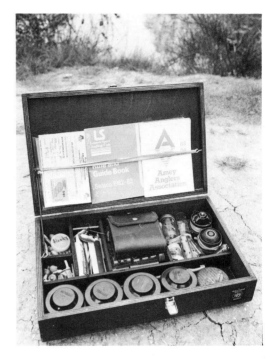

Carry your membership cards and licences somewhere safe and handy. It is no good telling the bailiff you left them at home.

7 Tench

I must confess to a special affection for tench; I like catching them and was personally on hand to photograph and witness the former record specimen which weighed a fraction over 10lb. However, the way its captor Tony Chester catches fish from large reservoirs and how I hunt them down in small gravel pits is vastly different – although both methods have been carefully matched to meet the demands of the venues we fish.

By tradition tench are a summer species, being the angler's target from the opening of the season in Mid-June through to late September. They do, however, feed right through the year but less fish are caught in the colder months. The biggest fish are likely to be hooked during the opening weeks of a new season, when many females may still be carrying up to a pound and a half of late spawn because the lead up to the normal spawning period has been delayed due to low water temperatures.

Once the females have shed their spawn they drop considerably in weight although generally they still outweigh their male partners, who often stick close to their 'wives' when hooked by an angler. It is not unusual for a fish to be played to the bank closely shadowed by its partner.

If you intend fishing really large waters like Tring where Tony Chester landed his massive fish, you only have one option as far as tackle set-ups go, and that's a long range leger rig and complicated bite indication system. Float fishing is generally out of the question because you won't be able to attain the range required, to present the bait properly or finally tell whether you have a bite or not.

The problem with fishing big open waters is that you won't have any idea of the underwater terrain. Ideally, gullies, drop-offs, edges of islands, channels and sand bars would at least give a series of possible fish holding areas. The reservoir angler usually faces a vast sheet of virtually unknown water with little first hand information to go on. It's often a matter of prospecting on a trial and error basis.

Most of the long range tench leger rigs I have fished with and seen have been simplicity themselves, except perhaps for a little doctoring of feeders to increase or decrease the exit of the groundbait or loose offerings. Knots are kept to a minimum – in fact they are not used at all. The main reel line runs right through to the hook, which varies from a 6 to 12, according to what bait you want to mount on it.

The best method is shown in the diagram. This clearly shows the simple set-up for catching tench at extreme range. The tail distance from hook and bait to feeder can vary from twelve inches to twenty-four inches. Don't use anything longer or the whole outfit will tangle up as it flies through the air.

To stop the feeder sliding down onto the bait a leger stop is attached to the line and

(Opposite) A quartet of specimen tench.

Buzzers are the name of the game in serious specimen hunting, but they are far from essential unless you fish long hours and all night.

Setting up for a tench session. Here is the full rig – Optonic buzzers, monkey climbers and sectional rod rests.

stopped by a tiny nylon plug. Don't make the mistake of jamming it home too tight; you won't be able to undo it and it could seriously damage the line.

By far the most popular feeder is the Drennan Feederlink, which is also probably the most doctored piece of fishing tackle on the market. Anglers take the basic tube and attack it with scalpels to enlarge its holes, glue leads in the bottom to make them cast better and even block off holes to impede the exit of baits like maggots.

However, the basic Drennan will catch fish. Once it is attached to the line the tiny cap at the top can be eased off and the tube filled with bait. The holes around the side will allow bait to escape once the feeder has hit the reservoir bed.

Although the rig is deadly, it can be improved upon in several respects. The feeder's bottom half can be taped shut. This is done when only a trickle feed is required in the target area. By experimenting with the number of holes blocked, bait leak can be delayed for many minutes.

Another feeder is designed to do the reverse. By enlarging some, or all of the holes, bait distribution can be rapid. Once the feeder is nearing the bottom of a swim, bait will be drifting out. And when it finally touches down it will empty almost immediately.

Drennan Feeders – and there are several sizes available – are notoriously bad fliers over long distances. The string of swan shot clipped to the bottom of each feeder is not especially aerodynamic and tends to flutter during a long cast.

Feeder 'flutter' is overcome by removing the swan shot completely and replacing them with an Arlesey bomb Araldited into a hole in the bottom. The bomb is mounted with the swivel end inside the tube. Leads

Attaching a monkey climber.

can vary in weights from ¼oz to 1oz.

A strong length of monofil line is attached to the swivel, passed through the existing Drennan cap and finally attached to a tiny brass ring link. Nose heavy feeders fly like a rocket.

All the feeders mentioned can be filled with maggots, casters, worms, hemp, and even solid groundbait, but you will have to dispense with the feeder caps, thus turning the tube into a mini open-end feeder.

A standard open-end feeder is usually made from clear plastic. The Drennan version is a green colour. Plugged with bait, the feeder empties its load soon after hitting the bed. A strip of lead is clipped to the outside of the tube to make it sink.

The feeder can be filled with plain groundbait, or a groundbait that's laced with hook bait offerings. Alternatively, a feeder can be stopped at one end with groundbait, filled with hook baits and plugged again at the opposite end with more groundbait.

Usually, the feeder is connected to the main reel line via a link of nylon line and a swivel. However, it's become standard practice to put a stiffener between the feeder and line to eradicate kinks and tangles when casting. This can be made from either a piece of stiff plastic or a length of silicone rubber slid over a stiff nylon link.

Block-ends are a lot simpler to use. They work the same way as an open-end feeder but are blocked off at each end with soft plastic caps. Both the previously mentioned feeders, which are sometimes known as 'plastic pigs', come in three sizes – large which make an almighty splash when they hit the water, medium and small, which are probably of more use.

If you know you are fishing a bottom that's covered with soft weed, then you will want to keep your bait out of the tangle so that a passing fish might see it. A stiff piece of copper wire is passed through a four or five inch long piece of silicone rubber. At one end is attached a swivel, which in turn is fixed to the main reel line, while the other end is attached to a bomb.

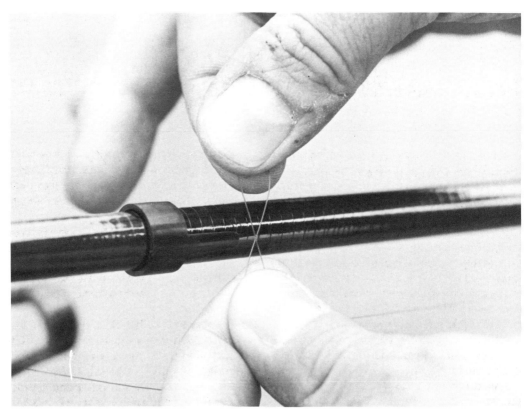

Plastic clip to hold line steady against wind or surface drag.

Plenty of backbone and easy action are essentials of a good tench rod, and are particularly valuable for big fish in weeded water.

Some anglers even attach a small cork near the swivel end of the rig to make sure it stands up.

For closer fishing, where balls of groundbait can be introduced into a swim either by a powerful catapult or by hand, a plainer hooking rig can be used. The simplest is a link leger. A short length of line, usually about 10lb, is doubled over and the required number of swan shot clipped to it. The main reel line is passed through the small nylon loop at the top and is stopped in the normal way with a leger stop. Alternatively a small snap link or John Roberts Link Leger bead is attached to the line and stopped in the normal way. The lead, normally a bomb with a swivel, is then clipped on.

The final long or medium range rig has a paternoster tail which can be up to 10 inches long. The beauty of this rig is that the taking fish cannot feel any weight on the line. A small swivel or leger bead can be used to attach paternoster line to main line.

Once a bait has been cast out the rod will have to be housed in a set of rod rests so that the bite indicators can be set up. Many tench anglers fish with two rods, so a double headed bar rest system will have to be used.

The double heads will take two rubber, non-slip, U rests to support the back ends of the rod handles, while the front bar will have threaded heads to take either straightforward Y heads for a running line, or Heron and Optonic electronic heads. I don't fish long sessions and rarely right through the night, so I don't fish with electric buzzer outfits. However, my rod

63

rest set-ups are very similar and the monkey climber arrangements are just the same.

The front double bar is set low, the final height being adjusted by a telescopic central rod. Rod tips should be low to present a low profile to any wind or breeze. The rear rod rests obviously have to be set a lot higher to achieve this effect.

Space the front and rear bars so that the rear forks are well clear of the reel. Position the front bar just a couple of inches in front of the first rod ring. Set the rod in place after casting and then push a stainless steel needle in the ground about three inches in front of the reel spool face. I like the end of the needle to terminate about two inches below the reel. Pull line from the spool downwards until it touches the ground at the base of the needle, and then slip a monkey climber over the steel rod until it traps the reel line. The reel bale-arm is then flicked open and a loop of line taken directly off the spool and clipped into a plastic line clip attached to the rod butt just in front of the reel.

When a tench picks up your bait and moves off, the monkey climber will travel up the needle, the movement matching the speed of the swimming fish. Once a clean take has been noted the rod can be picked up out of its rests, the reel bale-arm carefully closed and the hook set. A spectacular strike isn't required. Simply wind down on any slack line and lift the rod. The power of the outfit on the lift should set the hook.

As you firmly strike, the monkey climber will drop off its needle out of harm's way and you will be free to play the fish. The line clip above the open reel is a safety precaution in case you miss the monkey climber rising. Once the indicator reaches the top of the needle and falls, the line will continue tightening and finally pull clear of the clip. The fish will then be free to continue taking line. If the bale is kept closed there is a chance of the fish feeling resistance and dropping the bait, or of it hooking itself and dragging your outfit into the water.

Monkey climbers can be made from a variety of materials depending on the amount of wind and drift experienced. I use one to two inch pieces of white plastic overflow pipe with a deep groove cut in one end to trap the reel line. You can use tin foil when there's little breeze about, or a piece of clear plastic tube which can be linked into a circle and filled with lead shot to counteract flow and drift. A Beta light can also be inserted for night-fishing.

When a gale is blowing, a block of soft foam can be inserted in the first rod ring to stop the line being buffeted which can result in a false bite. Alternatively, a small line clip can be attached to the rod in front of the first ring. A fish will pull line free when it takes the bait.

For night fishing Beta lights can be taped to monkey climbers or inserted in clear plastic carriages which travel up and down the steel needles. It's surprising how the human eye can adjust to night vision and pick up the pale green glow.

Watching monkey climbers or bobbins is out of the question for the long-session and all-night tench fisherman who uses electronic bite alarms to give him an indication when a fish is running with a bait.

There are a number of models on the market, but the two most popular are the Heron and more sophisticated Optonic alarms. The Heron head which takes the place of the Y fork front rod-rest works by a simple wire antenna being pulled onto a

(Opposite) Dense reeds, plenty of cover and abundant natural food are the key features of a big tench water.

LANDING A BIG FISH

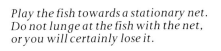

Play the fish towards a stationary net. Do not lunge at the fish with the net, or you will certainly lose it.

The fish slides into the meshes. Take it easy, and be prepared for a sudden dive.

Lift the net rim so that the fish settles into the meshes.

Pull the fish towards you, still in the water, then lift the net by the rim. Do not crank it out on the handle.

contact by the pressure of line as the fish takes. Once the electric circuit is completed a red light emitting diode flashes and a buzzer sounds off in a separate power box and amplifier, which is connected to the head by a lead.

The Optonic alarms are extremely popular and come in two types – one with built in battery supply and amplifier, or with indicator head and separate-power supply and buzzer box connected by a lead. The latter model is useful for the angler who sleeps at his swim. The buzzer control can then be sited right by the ear!

Optonic alarms are triggered off by moving line running over a wheel. As a fish takes the bait, the connecting spindle turns a paddle which breaks a beam of light as it revolves. This in turn sets off the alarm and LED.

Tench anglers, and most other specimen hunters, like this type of alarm because the amount and speed of buzzes and flashes can be interpreted. One bleep might mean a fish is nosing the bait, three bleeps and then nothing could indicate a dropped bait, while a steady or quickening series of bleeps or buzzes invariably means a

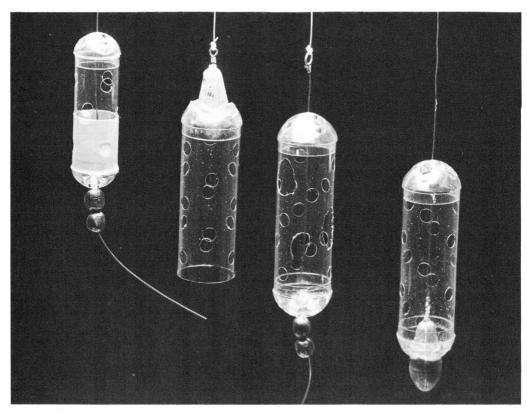

Standard and modified feeders. See text for details.

Close to 6lb Len Head checks the weight of a tench from a small stillwater fishery. Overall, any fish over 5lb is well worth having; even a 4lb tench is a prize for most anglers.

positive take.

I have gone into detail on rod rest set-ups, bite indicators and alarms in this chapter because the very same rigs will be used for catching carp, bream, big roach and pike.

Unlike carp fishing, offering a bait at a shoal of tench isn't that complicated. They are lovers of natural baits and will take bread, worms (lob and red), mussels, maggots, casters, sweetcorn, hemp and finally boiled high nutritional value (HNV) baits, if you can be bothered to prepare them.

The other way of catching tench from smaller gravel pits, lakes and ponds is probably more enjoyable and involves watching a float disappear, although link-leger, freelined and mini-feeder's outfits will also work on these types of venues.

Tench only feed through the day during mid-summer; even then bites can be slow around mid-day. The best periods are at the crack of dawn and from early evening until an hour after dark. In my experience tench never feed avidly for more than a few hours each day.

I like catching tench virtually under my rod top by clearing out a swim with a rake or fishing a pitch that's already been cleared and baiting it up with groundbait made from mashed bread, brown bread-crumbs, perhaps laced with maggots and worms. Don't go too heavy on the worms though; they have a habit of attracting eels!

If you're fishing a gravel pit, plumb the depth and find where the nearside shelf starts to drop away. This is where the tench will be patrolling. Groundbait the pitch and cast out a bottom end waggler type float or even a simple length of quill, fixed bottom end only. Shot the float down so that just the top shows, positioning the bulk of your lead so that it's sitting hard on the bottom. The tail, which can be up to a foot long, should be armed with a size 10 hook baited with a large lobworm, bunch of maggots or piece of breadflake.

Tench taken on a float do not muck about. The float will either go straight under (and this is the time to strike), or rise from the water and lie flat on the surface, which is caused by the fish lifting the cocking shot. Don't wait for it to sit up again – set the hook.

The tench is a big feeder and often travels around in a large shoal. First signs of feeding fish are a series of small bubbles breaking surface. If this happens in your swim be prepared for action. If there isn't much response don't pile in groundbait which will sour the pitch. Sit tight and wait – tench don't travel far and they will come back.

Lake swims can be tackled much in the same way, although lakes have fairly uniform depths and finding a patrolling ridge might prove more difficult. In this case, fish up tight against a patch of lilies – it always produces fish for me. Flick out loose feed and small balls of groundbait right on the edge of the pads and lure the fish out.

8 Carp

Catching carp has been turned into a science by the many thousands of anglers who specialise in catching these powerful and beautiful fish. Techniques and bait selection are probably the most comprehensive in the whole field of coarse fishing. But putting your first double figure fish on the bank doesn't have to be that complicated.

There are two very simple ways of catching carp; spotting individual or shoals of fish and then setting out to hook the specimens you have seen; or fishing blind in a known fish holding area which you have previously pre-baited, and then waiting for the carp to come to you.

The first method is exciting and brings out the natural sporting element although it can prove frustrating when a fish, clearly in view, won't take a bait cast right in front of its nose. The sitting it out and waiting method also yields carp providing you have the time and patience.

Before setting out to hook a fish that has been tracked down you will have to equip yourself with a couple of essential items, namely a pair of polarising glasses which will enable you to see free swimming fish more clearly in the water, and a good pair of binoculars. These are used to scan the water surface, hoping to pick out the black tell-tale shapes of carp just under the surface. The glasses will also prove useful to watch other anglers!

Carp generally follow the same patrolling routes through the summer months. So it will pay to spend a few hours stalking them before you even attempt setting up your tackle. Make a mental note of where

fish will be lying at given times of the day, how many fish are in a shoal, and if they appear to be feeding on surface snippets or just cruising about.

Carp are easy enough to spot. They often create bow waves as they cruise and the peculiar 'clooping' sound they make as they suck in surface food is a giveaway. Polarising glasses will cut down water surface glare, enabling the angler to see the fish more clearly. Fish cruising at a distance can be picked up more easily through binoculars.

Once you think you have enough information it's time to set out to catch them. We have already talked about rods, reels and line, which is all the gear you will probably want other than half a dozen spare hooks and a large landing net.

Bait for most surface carping is either bread, which I favour; special 'floaters', which is nothing more than a cake based on soya flour, colours, sweeteners and eggs baked in the oven for thirty minutes, or buoyant meat-based foods intended for cats. The bait list can also include buoyant boilie baits, but for the purpose of this exercise, a fresh loaf of crusty bread will suffice.

On arrival at the water, tackle up well away from the bank. Pull off a chunk of bread crust about the size of a golf ball, and mount it on a size 4 or 6 hook of your choice. Head for the area where you believe the fish to be, and keep as quiet as possible as you reach the water's edge. The slightest noise will scare the carp. Once the target fish, or shoal, has been spotted gently dip the lump of bread briefly in the

water. This will allow the bait to absorb a small amount of water, making it heavier and easier to cast. Flick out the bait as close to the fish as you can . . . and wait!

Carp are suspicious fish and generally don't slam into a bait. They often swim gently up to the offering and nose it, sometimes deliberately giving it a nudge, just to check it out . . . be ready for anything.

I have been caught out many times by fish that have slammed into a bait and left me wondering what had happened. One moment the bait floats untouched, the next, the water surface erupts as a carp sucks the bread cleanly off the hook.

Fishing floating baits is a cat and mouse method and you have to be as crafty and patient as the fish. Keep an eye on your bait at all times, even if it's floating under your rod top. Carp aren't fussy if they have it in their mind to take a bait, no matter where it is. I have caught carp at my feet on floating bread.

Your rod should be held at all times. Once the fish takes the bait, whether it be a screaming run or just a gentle pluck, lift the rod cleanly upwards and set the hook. Don't let the fish run with the bait before striking. Waterlogged bread is very soft and a hook can fall from it very easily.

Catching carp from a baited swim is rather more complicated and involves working out where you think carp might be lying, presenting a high protein or particle bait from a massive range available and fishing it on a seemingly complicated terminal rig. Like fishing with floating baits, you must know where the fish will be feeding. Once you have pinpointed a target area the next job is to introduce some baits – the same kind you will be later fishing on a hook.

This is where you 'pays your money and makes your choice' because the bait possibilities range from naturals like worms and meat-based attractors through to special 'boilies' which are the most consistent carp catchers. One carp bait supplier lists no less than twenty-three basic 'boilie' ingredients; forty-five liquid flavours, including apple, rabbit, menthol and wedding cake!; plus eight types of particle baits, like hemp, tares and peas; not forgetting a range of half a dozen different dyes, sweeteners, taste stimulators and liver extract.

All the above basic carp protein mixes and additives are well proven but for the middle of the road angler it might be best to start off by fishing carp boilies made by the angler from a range of ready mixed baits like those marketed by Geoff Kemp Bait Ingredients, Richworth Baits or Catchum Baits and Flavours.

Current baits and flavours marketed by Richworth Baits

READY MIX PROTEIN PACK
50% Protein Content
Available in:
1lb pack
5lb pack
10lb pack

CONCENTRATED SWEETENER
5 ml = 2lb sugar
Available in:
Clear 1lb bottle
Dense 1lb bottle
Clear 50ml bottle (about ½lb)
Dense 50ml bottle (about ½lb)

(Opposite) Big carp are much more of a challenge, demanding time, effort and sometimes plenty of cash. Len Head's mirrors weighed in at 20 and 29lb and were the result of hours of hard work.

ASSORTED COLOURINGS
Specially sweetened 8oz pack
Available in: Brown Black Green
Blue Yellow Red

ASSORTED FLAVOURS
1000:1 concentration
Available in: 1lb or 50ml
(about ½lb) bottles

Strawberry	Apple
Creamy Toffee	Vanilla
Rum and Butter	Cherry
Walnut	Jasmin
Blackcurrant	Maple
Roast Beef	Peach
Coconut	Butter
Aniseed	Gooseberry
Rhubarb and Custard	Raspberry
Roast Peanut	Caramel
Fruit Cocktail	Cheese
Liquorice	Hazelnut
Apricot	Tangerine
Baked Bread Crust	Guava
Water Melon	Lemon
Cream	Leather
Smoky Bacon	Blue Cheese
Concord Grape	Spearmint
Burnt Sugar	Sweetcorn
Sage and Onion	Greengage
Quince	Cranberry
Lemon	Banana
Bun Spice	Rum and Raisin

Boilies 1 – Mix the eggs and flavouring.

Carp anglers favour boiled baits for two reasons. They don't break up very quickly in the water and have a useful fishing life of well over three hours; and they can't be nibbled away by smaller 'nuisance' fish like bream and roach. Tench also are known to have a sweet tooth for carp baits.

Hard skinned boiled baits can be fired long distances in powerful catapults. Carp men continuously fire boilies into target areas well over sixty-five yards, although it's worth remembering that only a trickle of baits should be introduced when the weather is cold and fish slow to feed.

For ease, I have chosen the Richworth Baits to illustrate the mixing, rolling and boiling techniques, methods which have put a string of 30lb carp on the bank in recent seasons. However, all bait mixes on the market have a very high success rate.

The only tools required for making up a pound of bait, enough for between 200 and 250 baits, will be a mixing bowl, spatula, pair of scissors, set of scales and a saucepan preferably with a wire basket. An old chip pan makes an ideal tool.

I will keep the mixing sequence simple by doing all the tasks by hand. An electric mixer can be used to blend the mix, but I shall outline the correct mixing drill so that it can be carried out on the bank, if required.

Boilies 2 – Blend the mixture with the base mix.

Boilies 3 – The flavoured paste ready for rolling.

Take six large eggs and crack them into the mixing bowl – these will act as a binding agent. Once the eggs are thoroughly beaten, add a heaped teaspoon of colouring which is sweetened. Richworth favoured red and yellow colourings, which they say can easily be spotted by patrolling fish.

Next comes the essence of your choice, say strawberry. This is very highly concentrated having a 1,000 to 1 strength. Just 5ml, half a capful, should be added to the mix. Pour in 5ml of sweetener, which comes in two types: thin for winter fishing when rapid leak is required; thicker mix for summer fishing when the water temperature is higher and a slower leak rate is needed.

Note: Sweeteners are powerful. A 5ml measure is equivalent to 2lb of sugar. Too much can actually repel rather than attract.

Beat the whole mix with a fork until everything is blended, then add a pound of the powdered 50 per cent protein mix. These mixes have been specially formulated to give the fish a balanced diet of important ingredients like sodium caseinate and soya flour.

Using the wooden spatula, fold in the ingredients until the mix is doughy. If the mixture still feels wet, add slightly more powder. Once it binds, take it from the bowl and continue kneeding by hand.

Pull off lumps the size of a golf ball and roll into a rough sausage shape. When the whole batch has been rolled out, take a plastic ice-cream tub and use the bottom to roll out the rough shapes into longer half inch sausages.

Boilies 4 – Break the ball into fat sausages, then roll each one into a thin strip.

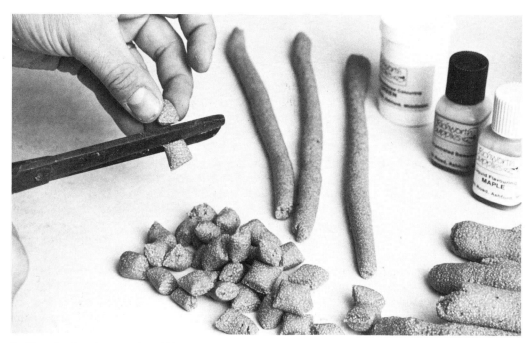

Boilies 5 – Cut the paste into ½in sections and roll them by hand into balls.

When the whole mix has been rolled out, cut them into half inch long pieces which are then rolled in the hand into half inch balls. Put the saucepan on the stove and bring to the boil. By now you should have between 200 and 250 soft paste baits ready for the boiling water.

(A neat bait balling tool has just come on the market. It works like an ice-cream scoop but has two cups. It is pressed in the fresh bait mix and squeezed to form a perfectly round ball of bait ready for the saucepan.)

The balls should be boiled vigorously for several minutes to form the vital tough skin. Finally lift the baits out of the water and tip them onto a towel and leave to cool, giving them a shake just to remove any excess moisture. If the above steps are carefully followed it should be possible to make 250 baits in just thirty minutes.

When fishing time is precious, ready mixed and moulded baits like the Len Middleton Specials are a boon. The baits, which are about the same size as the half inch home prepared rolled boilies, come in self-sealing packs of forty-four baits and can be plucked off like beads as required. For ease they can be stored in a freezer and taken out prior to a carp fishing session.

Each bait is made up of eleven different ingredients and the packs come in three types: high protein, carbohydrate or a balanced mix of both. The sealed packs can also be sprayed with additional attracting flavours from an atomiser. Each pack of specials sells for around £1.45.

The other baits that the serious carp angler should try are particle or multiple baits like the well-tried and tested sweetcorn, plus a whole variety of beans including broad, black eyed, red kidney and mung, plus maple, dun and chick peas. Not forgetting hemp, peanuts and even lupin seeds! All these baits can be coloured

Boilies 6 – Boil the baits to toughen the outer layer.

and even flavoured.

One word of warning about fishing with bean and dried seed baits. If not cooked before being put on a hook they could germinate and actually harm the carp. The rule is to boil these baits for a couple of minutes to avoid any risks.

So now we have the tackle and the baits – next comes the terminal rigs. This is a science and for the purpose of this book I shall explain just two, the hair and bolt rigs, both of which have proved to be deadly.

A whole chapter could be written about the development of the 'hair', but suffice to say that it was designed jointly by Kevin Maddocks and Len Middleton to tempt shy biting fish to take a bait. Full credit must go to them and I will describe their original rig which has been copied many times

Hundreds of stillwaters now offer plenty of action with carp up to 15lb. Easy to catch, they are a perfect target for the beginner.

and adapted to suit other situations.

The basic 'hair' is a method of fishing either a particle or boilie bait *off* the hook. The hook is tied to the main line as described in the chapter dealing with knots. A short length of 1lb monofilament line is then tied to the shank of the hook with a half hitch on the bend. Some anglers tie the 'hair' to the eye of the hook.

The light line (hair) is threaded through the eye of a fine sewing needle which is then passed through the boilie or particle bait. Particles can be fished singularly or in multiples; boiled baits can be fished as singles, ones or twos or even halves and quarters, strung out along the hair.

Once passed through the bait(s) the hair is removed from the needle and the trailing

end doubled back, tied off and trimmed neatly. Despite the seeming frailty of the hair, it can be cast long distances without fear of it flying off.

Terminal rigs vary from angler to angler. A typical long range rig would be made up of twenty yards of 12lb to 15lb leader line tied to the main reel line, this is to avoid crack-offs when casting to distant swims.

A link swivel or John Roberts leger bead is threaded onto the leader or main line and stopped with a barrel swivel. To this swivel is attached the hook bottom which can be made from line strengths ranging from 6lb to 8lb, heavier line being for waters where bigger fish roam.

The sliding link or leger bead is used so that differing weights of bomb can be attached quickly and simply without the need of having to break down the whole rig. For long distance casting 3oz Arlesey type leads are used, 2oz and 1oz being more useful for closer range fishing. The leads can be fixed direct to bead or fished on nylon links varying in length from three to six inches long.

A bolt or shock rig, as it is sometimes called, has been developed to deal with bold biting fish. It works on the principle that the fearless fish picks up the bait, swims off, feels the lead and panics. As it tries to bolt free the main line is pulled up short and the hook set.

Setting up a bolt rig is very much the same as the hair. The only difference is that a stop is fixed between four and six feet above the lead. It can be made either from a conventional stop knot and bead or plastic leger stop. As the fish takes line it is free to do so until the stop hits the eye of the bomb. Then the line tightens and the fish can be hit.

(Opposite) A big gravel pit carp comes to the net. Take your time and play the fish out before you attempt to land it.

Some anglers don't use the stop-knot system at all, preferring to fish the main line very tight from bomb to rod which is clipped securely in rests. Both ideas are based on the same principle which only works on stillwaters where carp are bold takers.

Rods and bite alarms are set up along the same lines as those mentioned in the chapter on tench fishing. For short sessions electronic buzzer alarms aren't really needed. These are more of a boon to the night and long session angler.

However, there are a couple of subjects that should be mentioned and the first concerns beefing up Optonic alarms. This clever piece of equipment has been designed to give the angler an indication that a fish has picked up his bait and is moving off. The loudness is deemed by the manufacturers to be sufficient, and this applies to both the compact and lead models.

Some anglers, however, like to sleep instead of fish, and to cut down on the number of missed runs they beef up their alarms so they would wake the dead. The result is a never ending stream of loud buzzes through the night as alarms are triggered by line bites, drifting weed, unsuspecting water birds fouling the line and anglers who can't stop playing with their toys.

The other unsporting element which is creeping into carp fishing is the diabolical practice of leaving rods still fishing while the angler is away from the swim. There have been cases where anglers have tied rods to rod rests to stop them being pulled into the lake, while reel bale arms have been left open so that a biting fish can take as much line as it wants. When the angler finally returns to his swim he hopes that a fish will have hooked itself in his absence.

Boilies 7 – Even though the bait seems hard, it is quite soft and palatable on the inside.

Behaviour of this kind is to be deplored, and water bailiffs should be given the power to impound tackle left unattended in this manner.

Long range carp fishing can have its special problems. The first is getting a bait to the same spot as the bait on the hook. Obviously, light carp baits can't be thrown sixty yards plus by hand and have to be fired out in a special catapult. Most modern carp anglers use target type catapults which have very small leather strip pouches. Normal catapults, like those used to fire out maggots and groundbaits, are not suitable for long range feeding with small compact baits. When firing a catapult some allowance must be made for the

(Opposite) Crucian carp. A small species of carp, but a hard fighter and willing feeder.

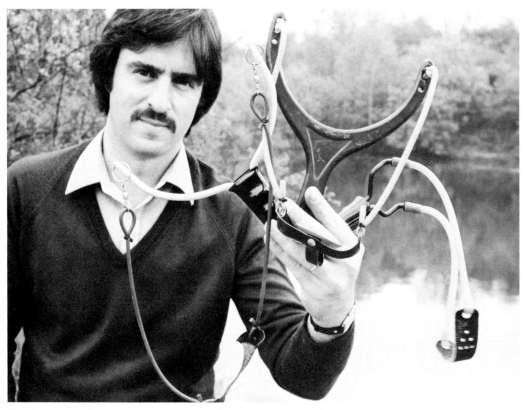

Feeding is very important for success. At long range, catapults are the only way to drop boilies and other baits into the target zone.

bait when it reaches the full extent of its range, as it's likely to flutter especially when a breeze is blowing.

Carp bites are usually rattlers. Monkey climbers fly up needles, buzzers bleep a warning and lines go tight up to their clips, sometimes even pulling free, allowing the line to spill from the spool. As the fish takes line, trip the bale arm and lift firmly into the fish. The power and weight of the moving carp against the power of the rod is often enough to set the hook. If you are fishing at extreme range then it would pay to take a step backwards and slam a little harder into the fish.

Carp are generally excellent fighters that boil and dive all the way to the bank. If you have the misfortune to get hung-up on an underwater snag don't pull the line in the hope of pulling free. Often the line

will part and leave the fish with your hook still trailing from its mouth. Ease off the pressure, open the bale arm and wait. If you are lucky the fish will swim free from the snag of its own accord. There are occasions, however, when a fish will snag you permanently, then it's a case of firmly pulling to free the fish and tackle.

Carp are big fish so land them in a large landing net. Don't use a knotted mesh. Choose one of the softer micromesh nets, and a net head with arms that are at least thirty inches long. Keep the net ready made up and close at hand. Once the fish shows signs of tiring bring it steadily to the net, which should be fully submerged. Guide the carp over the net, never try to stab at it with the landing net – the carp will panic and you will probably lose it.

Once the fish is clearly over the net area,

gently lift the frame to engulf the catch and draw it towards you, finally enmeshing the fish completely. Don't try to lift a carp from the water but continue pulling it towards you, finally grabbing the net at the spreader before lifting.

Carp have tough leathery mouths but hooks can usually be removed quite quickly with the aid of a pair of artery forceps. If the fish must be weighed, use a proper weigh-sling that's been thoroughly wetted. And if the carp must be retained, use a special nylon carp sack with sufficient air holes punched into it.

The above mentioned methods and baits are designed to catch common, mirror and leather carp. The smaller crucian carp can be caught on the tackle, baits and methods outlined in the roach and rudd fishing chapter.

9 Bream

Match anglers who draw on a productive bream hole know they have the competition sewn up if they tackle the swim the correct way. Specimen hunters, on the other hand, have always classed the species as vermin! Specimen hunters scorn bream because of the way marauding shoals pick up expensive special baits presented for carp and tench. In recent seasons, however, their attitude has changed dramatically. Today a 10lb plus bream is what every specimen hunter wants chalked up on his trophy sheet. The surge of interest has been sparked off by a worked out gravel pit alongside the A40 Oxford by-pass, which holds a remarkable stock of bream well in excess of 10lb. The current record breaker of 13¾lb came from the very same water, known as the Thames Conservancy or TC Pit.

Bream don't have to be that big to be a sporting proposition; but it would be fair to point out that the species isn't known for its fighting capabilities. Find a shoal and net out half a dozen five pounders during the course of a day and I reckon you have had a good day's sport.

Gravel pits and lakes invariably hold the better size fish, which can easily be caught on leger or float tackle. Float gear is without a doubt the most enjoyable rig to fish but leger tactics often account for more fish.

Bream tackle is simplicity itself. Groundbaiting, feeding and bite interpretation are more critical. Get any of the vital disciplines wrong and you could scare the shy fish out of the swim.

Leger tackle usually consists of either standard or doctored Drennan Feederlinks, like those described in the chapter on tench fishing, open-end feeders, or a straightforward fixed paternoster. Main line should be 4lb straight through, but it might pay to beef up the monofil to 5lb if fishing a particularly snaggy swim. One useful rig is a converted Drennan that has a bomb glued in the back, and the nose cap removed and temporarily plugged with groundbait to hold in loose feed. The feeder is fixed direct to the line, while a weaker hook length of 3lb line twelve inches long is tied above. Hooks can be either a 14 or 16.

The rig can fail on two vital points. Because the lead is positioned in the back of the feeder it won't fly very well after casting, and it isn't really large enough to carry the high amount of feed demanded by bream. The rig will work, however, if the angler can introduce further groundbait either by hand or catapult. A large stiff catapult pouch, usually made from plastic, holds the soft groundbait which is lobbed into the swim. The bait must not be compressed prior to firing.

Another rig that's similar is the paternoster outfit. This is set up as the previous tackle but the feeder is replaced by an Arlesey bomb which can vary in weight from ¼oz to 1oz. This is a super outfit for

(Opposite) A netful of bream this size are big news for the matchmen. It's not unknown to build a 100lb plus bag in three or four hours.

*Groundbaiting is an essential tactic in bream fishing to attract
and hold the shoals.*

*Maggots – coloured and whites. These are a staple bait for most
stillwater species. Casters also are first rate fish attractors.*

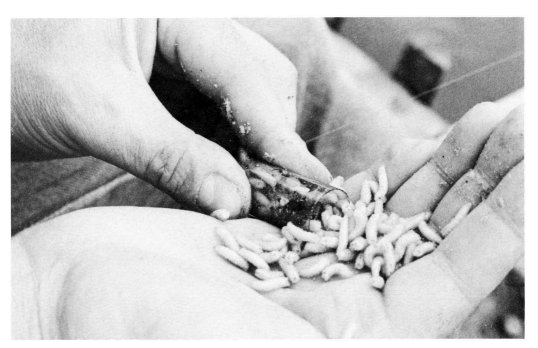

Loading a feeder 1 – Block the end of the tube with groundbait, then push in a portion of maggots.

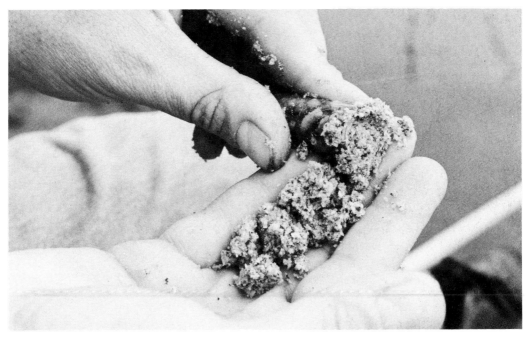

Loading a feeder 2 – Seal the maggots inside with a second plug of groundbait. Now the rig can be cast quite hard without losing its load.

fishing medium range when balls of groundbait can be fired or thrown out accurately by hand to the target area.

The rig I personally favour is a medium open-end feeder attached direct to the main line. I like fishing with it for a number of very important reasons. First, I don't have to fish with a weaker paternoster tail. As I have already said knots are weak links – and weak links can mean lost fish.

Secondly, the medium open-end carries quite a lot of feed which means I still have a chance of attracting a fish to my baited hook if I miss the main target area by a couple of feet.

Thirdly, a loaded open-end is quite weighty and will cast very long distances. Beware using the largest size feeders, though. Loaded, they hit the surface like half a house brick.

And finally, the free travelling line and hook is in positive contact with the rod tip. When the bream bites there is a direct pull between the fish and my right hand which is resting on the rod at all times.

The rig is simple enough to make. The main reel line is passed through the swivel attached to the feeder and is stopped about eighteen inches above the hook with a leger stop.

For some reason bream like cocktail (multiple) baits. A single maggot will attract fish but two maggots and a brandling seems to work better. Worm and caster is another scoring combination as is one maggot, caster and brandling, a small lively red worm found in compost heaps. Some anglers favour bread but I have no confidence in it for long range bream fishing because I can never be sure the bait is still on the hook after making the cast.

Groundbait is a must for breaming. It not only holds the fishes' attention but acts as a vital hook sample carrier. But get the mix wrong and you could be in

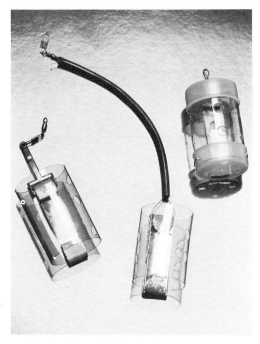

Standard and tangle-free feeders.

trouble. A sloppy mix won't ball-up and a dry mix will break up in mid-flight.

My method is as follows. Take a shallow bowl and pour in a good measure of dry brown breadcrumbs and then, using an empty bait box as a ladle, add water to the dry mix. Never add groundbait to water. Gently stir in small measures of water while swishing the bait around with your fingers. The trick is to work in the water while keeping the mix fluffy.

The final mix should be moist and you can tell when it's right by firmly squeezing a handful. If it balls up firm then it's perfect; if it's cloggy then you are either using a poor quality groundbait that's laced with greasy biscuit crumbs or you have added too much liquid.

Groundbait is basically a bait *carrier*. However, you must be careful how many

Nobody knows more about tench fishing than Len Head.
Here's proof. Actually, he was fishing for carp at the time.

Barry Waldron fishes the margins for perch.

Perch are making a strong come-back now that disease is on the decline. Soon we should see more of the big 3 and 4lb fish of years gone by.

*A small private gravel pit, early June and a big carp on the
bank. What more could you ask for?*

Bomb and link leger attachment for bream fishing without the feeder.

Quiver tips – the best all-round indicator for feeder fishing for bream.

hook samples are added to a mix. Maggots are alive and will break up a ball of bait before it reaches a swim. Worms are no problem, and you can add as many casters as you like.

As a rule prime bream hookbaits like gozzers, which are home-bred white maggots, and commercial maggots are not mixed into groundbaits. It is more usual to add the smaller and inferior pinkies, so called because of their pale pink colour, and squatts.

Never overfeed a swim from the start. Work up the pitch gradually and as the bream respond steadily add more groundbait. If the fish don't come, don't make the mistake of 'filling' in the swim – it will sour completely.

Many contraptions have been invented for spotting bream bites, but I keep it sim-

ple by using a quiver tip. This is nothing more than a sensitive tip which is permanently built into or screwed into the end of a nine foot leger rod. It's made from solid glass fibre or carbon and responds to the slightest touch when a bream takes a bait.

And this is the main problem when bream fishing. Bream mill about searching for food usually nose down. They are so pre-occupied that they often swim into the line, giving a perfect bite indication back on the bank.

Bites can vary from the faintest quiver to a belting take with the tip pulling right round. Liners, drop back and true bites all have to be struck at because you don't know what's happening to your hook and bait.

To get the best bite indication, the

Slightly down-turned mouth and extendable lips mark the bream as a bottom feeder that sucks its way through mud and debris.

angler should sit at almost right angles to the bank. The rod should be positioned on a forward rod rest and held at all times in the right hand, finger lightly resting on the reel spool. Once the cast has been made it's best to reel down on the leger or feeder slightly to set the quivertip; i.e. tension it under gentle pressure. When a bream finally takes the bait the tip will be pulled around farther.

Catching bream on the float at medium and long range is a most enjoyable way of fishing. A waggler, or bottom attached float, is set so that the bait is just sitting on the bottom or with a lightly shotted tail laying on the lake or gravel pit bed.

The rig is simple enough. Reel line is 4lb and can go right through to the hook, which is either a 16 or 18 if the fish are bold biters. If the fish are shy it will pay to scale down the hook bottom, the last couple of feet of line, to 3lb or even 2½lb.

A 2 swan waggler – a float needing two of the largest split shot to cock it – is ideal for long range bream fishing because of the way the tackle is balanced. The float is held in place with locking shot, one above the float, and the rest tightly grouped below. This arrangement ensures that the float travels like a dart when cast. Lighter shot are strung along the line to get the bait down quickly.

Hook baits are the same as for legering but because you won't be carrying groundbait and loose feed in a feeder, it will have to be introduced by hand or catapulted out into the swim, as previously described.

On the right tackle bream can offer good sport. They won't fight as hard as tench and usually come in quietly.

10 Roach & Rudd

Roach and rudd from just a few ounces and up through the magical 2lb barrier are a pleasing fish to catch; they fight hard for their weight and are attractive to look at once lying safely in the landing net. Fish approaching the 3lb mark and above are rare specimens for the average angler, who would do far better to set his sights on fish scaling around a pound and upwards to 2lb.

To catch the really big roach from large reservoirs and gravel pits the angler can use exactly the same gear as he would for tench fishing, which has already been fully explained. But for the smaller, but none the less worthy specimens, I would recommend a much lighter floatfishing outfit – and this is where a stiff actioned carbon float rod and medium sized but fast retrieve reel can play a vital role. Roach are mid-water and bottom feeders which can be found patrolling just a couple of rod lengths from the bank or right out in the middle of a lake. If they are close-in, you're in luck, as they can be taken on relatively light float gear.

For the purpose of this exercise let's assume they are feeding six rod lengths out and tackle up accordingly. If you find them closer in it's simple enough to scale down the size and shot carrying capacity of your float to cope with the situation. Because we want to be able to cast a long way we shall pick a 3AAA (or 1½ swan) bottom-only fixed waggler float. The large amount of lead needed to set the float will enable the relatively powerful rod to punch the gear as far as we require.

Main line will be 3lb and the float will be set so that the bait is just brushing the bottom of the lake or pit, if it's not too deep. One of the AAA shot will be nipped on the line in the exact position you want the float to ride. A second shot will be sited immediately the other side of the float ring. This leaves us with exactly 1 AAA to play with. This can be split up into smaller shot like 2 BB or 4 No. 8. I would probably pinch one of the BB on the line halfway between float and hook, while stringing a couple of No. 8s equally below.

The idea of breaking down the shot in a decreasing scale is to get the bait sinking more slowly as it reaches the bottom. This is because roach will often take feed 'on the drop' or before it finally settles. If we sited most of our lead low down near the hook we wouldn't be able to cast properly (the low bulk shot would tangle the main reel line during the cast) and we wouldn't get a slow descent of the bait.

For roach fishing a fine wire hook, size 16 is ideal. Roach are chunky, thick-set fish and can easily throw a small fine hook; however, if the fish prove hard to tempt it will pay to scale down to an 18. On the other hand if you keep bumping fish (fail to contact) then scale up to something with more hooking power. A hook like the Mustad barbless crystal 90340 is a good choice.

Roach eat most things dangled in front of them but white or coloured maggots, casters and worms are all excellent attractors. Bread can be used but I confess to having no confidence in it, especially where long range float fishing is concerned. In general, roach are slow to

Matchman Dave Fackrall sharpens up
his roach technique on a late season
visit to Ardleigh reservoir.

Match rod and float rig is a sporting
roach tactic at short–medium range.
Len Head's second rod is set up with a
long-range feeder. He uses a buzzer
instead of a quiver tip.

respond to angler's bait and it might take
an hour of steady but thoughtful feeding to
get them to respond. Even then the bites
can be 'fragile'.

Feeding can play an important part in
getting the fish to respond and I start out
by catapulting up to a dozen maggots into
the swim on every cast. Small balls of pure
brown breadcrumb, perhaps laced with
maggots or casters, can be added at the
same time. Once the fish begin feeding and
roach start coming to hand it's time to
draw the pre-occupied shoal closer towards you. This is done by gradually reducing the fishing and feeding range.
Never draw the fish too close, though.

Two to three rod lengths is ample.

Fishing a float at long range can be a
problem when there's a stiff wind blowing
across the front of an angler. The breeze
can pick up a floating line and drag the
float off station. The easiest remedy is to
soak the reel spool overnight in washing-
up detergent prior to fishing which re-
moves the greasy film of the line enabling
you to sink it after casting. Overcast the
feeding area, wind down on the float
rapidly with the rod tip under the water.
This pulls the float into the correct position and sinks the line under the surface
out of harm's way.

A very effective way of picking up roach

(Opposite) The result of an hour's
fishing on the feeder.

Hit the shoal at the right time, and you could fill a net with prime roach like these.

94

Specimen stillwater rudd.

is to fish a 'balanced' bait, one that hangs in the water or sinks ultra-slowly as it nears the bottom. This can be done by fishing with an air-filled bait like casters. Take a handful of casters and put them in a bait tin filled with water. Some will float, others sink. Select a couple that float, mount them on the hook and cast out. Initially the bait will sink quickly as the BB shot pulls them down. Then the bait will slow right down for the last couple of feet of descent and prove irresistible to the roach. If you feel the bait is sinking too quickly for those last vital feet, slide the lightest bottom shot halfway up the rig. If

bites prove hard to get switch to an ultra-light hook bottom. Go as light as 1½lb to get fish – the tackle may look frail but it can handle most roach.

Rudd are predominantly surface feeders so a slightly different approach will have to be adopted to catch these splendid fish, which often give their positions away at the crack of dawn by pimping on the surface. The pimps, or rings, are formed by the fish feeding on insect life in the surface film. During the day, when there's generally more breeze, it's hard to spot the surface feeders unless it's unusually calm.

The roach gear already outlined will

Melvyn Russ set up for roach on the feeder rig. Note that his rod rest angles along the bank so that it holds the rod at a sharp angle to the line. That way, the quiver tip is much more sensitive.

form the basis of our rudd gear, although it will differ slightly from float to hook. A waggler float, either straight or bodied, will be the casting weight and means of keeping the bait up near the surface. Loading will depend on how far you have to cast. Generally rudd are distant feeders so something like a 3 BB might not seem unreasonable. Where the outfit differs from the roach rig is that *no* shot are strung down the line and the bait is initially fished mid-water.

The bait must be allowed to gently float or 'hang' in the water so that the higher feeding rudd will have time to scent it and home in. By picking the right baits, like buoyant casters (floaters) matched with maggots, it is possible to make a bait hover near the surface.

Rudd are bold feeders and can be offered large amounts of loose feed with little fear of scattering the often huge shoals. A large soft pouched catapult will be needed to fire out the feed, which should be introduced every other cast.

One little dodge I learnt from a fellow angler while fishing Weirwood reservoir in Sussex, is to lace groundbait with floating casters. Once the ball sinks the buoyant hook bait samples break free and float up to the waiting rudd. It's a method that sends the rudd crazy.

Rudd can get so carried away with feeding that they almost anticipate the feed coming and jump out of the water when the bait hits the surface. When this happens set your rig shallower and pick the fish off the surface. The above methods will catch rudd, roach and crucian carp.

The species can be caught closer to the bank from less fished waters. If there are lots of reeds or bullrushes for cover then it may be possible to poke your tackle

Prime roach for stillwater. Despite all the talk about 2 pound fish by the dozen from some reservoirs, an average weight of between 12oz and 16oz is good going.

through the vegetation and pick the fish off as they patrol the margins. The float gear already mentioned can be used or you can fish with very basic tackle comprising a plain quill float, fished bottom only, with a few small shot clipped on the line to give you some casting ability. The float doesn't have to cock – it's purely a casting aid.

If you're lucky enough to have access to a water that contains very big rudd then the tackle will have to be beefed up. You can either upgrade the float rigs already outlined or fish with the bottom rigs described in the chapter on tench fishing.

11 Perch

My first big perch – I think it weighed nearly 1½lb – was caught by accident while fishing for small fish, mainly roach and gudgeon, in the River Lea at King's Weir, Hertfordshire. The rig was very simple, and it still works today.

I had been catching a stream of small fish, with the usual boyish enthusiasm, just a few yards out from the reed fringe banks, when out of the blue a large swirl engulfed the small gudgeon I was reeling to the surface. Naturally, I was excited and put the attack down to a hungry jack pike. The same thing happened while reeling in another fish but this time something compact and weighty had a firm hold of the livebait. Finally, the fish broke surface on that chilly winter's afternoon and I feasted my eyes on my first ever perch, an experience I haven't forgotten after twenty-five years.

Since those heady boyhood days, the country's perch population has been decimated by a mystery bacterial disease which even today top fishery biologists know nothing about. Luckily, perch have survived and are still a worthwhile proposition to the well equipped angler.

I would personally try to catch big perch on livebaits. I acknowledge that legered lobworms do lure fish, as do small spinners, but I prefer a live fish bait at all times. Perch aren't big fish but it would be folly to fish for them with ultra-light lines. They inhabit snaggy swims and there's always the likelihood of a fish bolting for cover and snagging you.

The rule is to fish with a suitably strong line to hold them on the run and a 4½lb to 5½lb monofil would be ideal. The float, used to suspend the livebait, can be any bulbous type. You can use a bubble, or heavy bodied waggler, or perhaps a very small pike pilot float. Anything will do as long as the livebait being fished can't pull it under.

Shot is clipped to the line to cock the float. It doesn't have to dot it low in the water – sufficient buoyancy should be left in the float to hold up the bait. The depth depends on the water being fished, but aim to have your bait swimming freely halfway between surface and bottom.

The hook is important. It should be fairly large, probably a size 4, 6 or 8 single, depending on the size of bait, and it must be forged for added strength. Wire hooks are of little use for perch fishing . . . they can pull out straight. Choose an eyed hook so that a good strong knot can be used to join hook to line. And a barbed hook will have to be used as it's the only way of keeping a live fish on.

Any small fish can be lip hooked as a bait but I have had most success on gudgeon, which are strong and lively, tiny roach and the best of all, minnows. These tiny fish make ace perch baits and in my opinion should be used in preference to all others.

(Opposite) Len Head with a netful of good fish taken on worm from the margins of a lily-bed.

Perch are rarely caught in clear open water, so seek a snaggy swim. Cast the tackle near overhanging bushes, sunken trees or spots where you know there is an underwater snag, for that is where the perch will probably be hiding. The perch is a bold biter. If it wants your bait it will swim up and grab it. The first thing you will know about it is the float either circling or disappearing from sight. Don't strike immediately but wait a couple of seconds and then set the hook.

All perch, no matter what size, fight hard. Don't expect to reel in straight away but be prepared to play it all the way to the bank. Once the fish is in the net be careful how you unhook it as the spiteful dorsal fin on the fish's back can pierce your skin. Once the fish is safely returned cast out to the same spot. Perch are generally a shoal

Perch rig. Polystyrene float, single shot and rudd livebait.

fish and if you can catch one there are usually several more swimming about in the area.

Perch can also be taken on simple paternoster tackle, comprising of main reel line through to a lead, usually a bomb. A short hook length holding a size 8 barbed hook armed with a worm is tied above. The other way of catching perch is to spin for them. Spinners imitate small fry or fish, and the flashing of the lure attracts the perch's attention. Again, 4lb or 5lb line should be used, and tied direct to a tiny, light spinner. Perch have very hard bony mouths but a wire trace isn't required to stop the line chafing through.

Spinners should be small, bright and flashy. The tiny Mepps Aglia lures, which range from ¾ inch up to just over an inch, are ideal for perch fishing. Colours are

Lobworm on the hook. Give him plenty of room to wriggle.

Look for dense weeds and lilies, and chances are there are perch around.

either gold or silver. The ABU Droppen blade spinners are equally good and come in weights from 2 gramme to 18 grammes. The smaller ones are more effective. Colours are copper, gold, silver, zebra pattern and fluorescent gold. Finally comes the Norwegian Dandy range made by Paravan, tiny spinner blade lures which come in a variety of colour combinations. The smaller lures are best, with the 4 and 6 gramme models being ideal.

Spinning is hard work as every sector of a swim has to be worked before moving onto a new spot. I work in an arc searching as much of a swim as possible. Perch will hit a spinner hard at all depths. Be prepared for the line to tighten as the fish strikes the lure. The ensuing fight is more than compensation for the arm tiring effort of working the lure.

12 Pike

Piking is the most exciting branch of still-water fishing. The thrill of battling it out with a double figure fish on balanced tackle is an experience that must be sampled to be believed. The fish are powerfully muscular, and from the moment the pike float submarines across the surface or the bobbin indicator dances up the needle the adrenalin starts to pump. You never know what size of fish has picked up the bait. A rattling take could be a kamikaze jack trying to swallow a bait that's far too large for its gullet; the slightest of twitches could be a twenty pounder teasing the bait before making the final attack.

Of all the forms of fishing available to the stillwater angler, piking is the ultimate challenge. The fish, unlike carp and tench, cannot generally be lured into a groundbaited area and then hooked. Pike have to be singled out and taken on a lonely fish bait or lure.

There are three basic ways of catching pike: fishing with livebaits, deadbaiting and lure fishing. Pike naturally live on live fish and I have no qualms whatsoever of catching them on these baits, although I also fish equally happily with deadbaits as well. Lure fishing is for the angler who has faith in the method. I have none after spending many hours fruitlessly casting large spoons, bar spinners and plugs into seemingly empty expanses of water. It may work for some anglers, but not for me. For my money you can't beat offering some form of fish bait to a pike. They are basically lazy fish, although they can rapidly home in on a fish if they feel so inclined. They prefer to take their time over a static or tethered meal before finally closing their jaws around it.

Mention should be made of the importance of fishing with a wire trace. It is folly to try and hook and play a pike on monofilament line. Pike have razor sharp teeth which can slice through nylon like butter – so a trace is a must. Shop bought traces are suitable but it's far better to make your own. Select 12 to 18 inches of cable laid wire, like Alasticum, and attach a small Berkley or Drennan swivel to one end. Pass the tag end through the eye twice and attach a pair of forceps to the trailing end. Then spin the forceps up a taut wire to form a neat, tight coil.

For most types of fish baits two hooks, either No. 8s or 10s, are attached to the other end of the wire. The first hook is attached via the eye, about 2½ inches up. The wire is then doubled back and passed through the eye for a second time before being wound round the entire shank. A second treble is then attached to the wire by passing the tag end twice through the eye and then spinning the spare end, the same way as attaching the swivel. In the name of conservation, many anglers use hooks that have two prongs without barbs, the third barbed leg being used to hold the bait. Crush the barbs flat with pliers.

(Opposite) Melvyn Russ puts back a 20 pounder.

There are four basic ways of presenting live or deadbaits to pike: floatfished free roving livebait or drifted deadbait; paternostered or tethered floatfished baits; sunken paternoster, and legered bottom bait. I have a lot of success with a free roving float rig. This comprises of a small traditional gazette float that has been rebuilt. I take the moveable wooden stem out and glue it back into place so that most of it is protruding from the bottom only. A wire eye is whipped to the end, resulting in a low profile float that can support a bait and drift with the wind.

The float's depth is set with a small plastic sleeve or bead and a stop knot at the required depth. The trace is attached to the line and weighted with swan shot clipped on the line just above the swivel. The rig is very simple and quite effective. Livebaits can be attached just as easily as deads. The higher hook is attached just below the dorsal tail root, while the leading treble can be fixed either in the lip or next to the tougher pectoral fin root.

Live coarse fish baits like roach, rudd, chub and gudgeon can be cast long distances, while frozen coarse deadbaits can be cast even further. However, fresh sea deadbaits, like sprats, can become soft and rip free from the hooks if cast too vigorously. They can be made more secure with a couple of turns of light nylon line. Frozen seabaits are no problem.

The traditional paternoster rig is very popular when a live bait has to be tethered in one particular spot, or when surface drift must be countered. Float choice varies from angler to angler. Some prefer the cigar type, either purchased from a shop or home made from eight inch lengths of balsa rod measuring about half an inch in diameter. Oversize pilot or drilled balsa or polystyrene ball floats, or even bulbous sliding floats are popular.

Whatever type you choose, it is stopped

Stillwater pike often congregate in the deep water around valve towers.

in the usual way with a bead and sliding stop knot. The end of the main reel line is attached to a swivel. A length of lighter 5lb line, called a rotten bottom, is attached to the same eye and an Arlesey bomb is attached to the free end. The trace wire and double set of treble hooks are attached to the free eye of the same swivel.

A slight variation on the rig, called a sliding paternoster, gives the livebait more freedom. The rig differs in that one eye of the swivel is attached freely to the main reel line. Stop knots and beads are positioned anything from a foot to three feet apart, depending on the depth of the water. This allows the livebait not only to work around the main line, but swim up and down as well. Some anglers call it the 'lighthouse' principle.

Another rig used extensively by pike

Assorted pike floats. Hollow plastic ball, balsa and converted Fishing Gazette design.

Roach bait on wire pike trace.

anglers is the sunken paternoster. Here a float is used to keep the bait up off the bottom but it is only used as a buoyancy aid and not as an indication of a pike taking the bait. The bait can be fixed or fished on a running line, again using a stop to prevent the free roving fish rising too high in the water. The float is also fixed in the normal free running way but the vital difference is that the bait is fished on a taut line. Bites are spotted by the bank angler with the aid of an electronic alarm or monkey climber outfit, with the line fished on an open reel spool and clipped up, the same system as used for carp fishing.

A boat angler doesn't normally fish with a fixed spool reel, preferring a small multiplier instead. The tackle is cast out and the line reeled firmly down on the bait. The spool is knocked out of gear but the ratchet left on. As the fish picks up the bait the ratchet ticks over the pawls as the fish moves off . . . working on the same principle as the Optonic electronic alarm.

The final terminal rig – and there are many variations to choose from – is the simple leger and freelined method used for presenting deadbaits. A bomb is attached freely by its eye to the line, followed by a small bead which acts as a buffer against the knot used to attach the line to trace. Alternatively, the lead can be omitted and the bait fished free.

However, a lead must be used if the bait is buoyant and fished off the bottom. This is done by cutting a small strip of high density polystyrene from an egg box and sliding it down the deadbait's throat. Or a small incision can be made in the

105

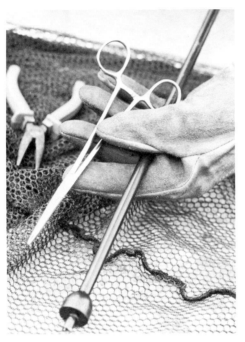

Pike surgery equipment. Pliers, forceps and long-handle disgorger. The glove is far better and kinder than a gag.

individually on a tray in the freezer overnight. Then the baits can be bagged up in dozens, and stored in tubs. It's a simple job to take out just the baits required for a day's sport, rather than having to try and prize open a frozen mass of fish.

The wind can be used to work baits into areas that are beyond normal casting distance. The free roving set-up already mentioned is used but the float has an additional vane attached to the top, which is designed to catch the wind. By picking your position it should be possible to get a bait to the most inaccessible spots. Some anglers attach small rubber balloons above their baits and then drift them out to the waiting fish.

Pike are peculiar fish. Sometimes you can crash through the undergrowth and almost drop baits on their noses, yet still

deadbait's vent and the polystyrene carefully pushed in the hole.

Deadbaits, which can be coarse fish or sea fish like sprats, smelt, mackerel or herring, are fished on the bottom and attached slightly differently to the livebaits previously mentioned. The higher hook, is pushed into the root of the tail and the forward hook dug into the flank. The forward part of the fish carries no hooks.

A word about deadbaits. It's a mistake to place a load of sprats, smelt (which make excellent baits because they give off a strong cucumber scent), herring mackerel, or coarse fish deadbaits straight in a freezer, because they come out as a solid unmanageable block. I have found it better to open-freeze them before packing in plastic bags and finally storing in old 4 litre ice-cream tubs. Place each fish

Livebait and deadbait traces stored on a roll of polystyrene.

Greed personified. Jack pike with a livebait almost too big to swallow.

catch fish. On other occasions they won't take a bait no matter how the tackle is presented. Broadland boat anglers always cut their outboard engines well before entering the fishing area. The commotion caused by the propeller would scare even the bravest fish. The rule, because of the shallow and sometimes clear water, is to tackle up outside the fishing area and then row to the swims with muffled oars. Bang-

ing about in a pike boat is frowned upon. The slightest bang is transmitted through the hull and water and will scare fish.

If fishing from a boat, don't forget to take an old piece of rubber carpet underlay or sack with you. Once you start fishing, wet it down and then as fish come aboard they can be laid in the bottom of the boat without fear of damaging the pike's scales or fins.

13 Handling your catch

All fish need careful handling once hooked. By following basic ground rules it should be possible to slip a fish back into the water unharmed.

Rule number one is never handle fish with dry hands. All fish are protected by a slimy mucus which shields them against skin infection. Wipe this away with dry hands and the fish is open to attack. Small fish can be swung to hand and the hook generally removed with the fingers. If the fish has taken the hook inside its mouth, or the point has become lodged in the throat, a barrel disgorger will have to be used to free it. On larger fish, or specimens that have tough mouths, a pair of artery forceps

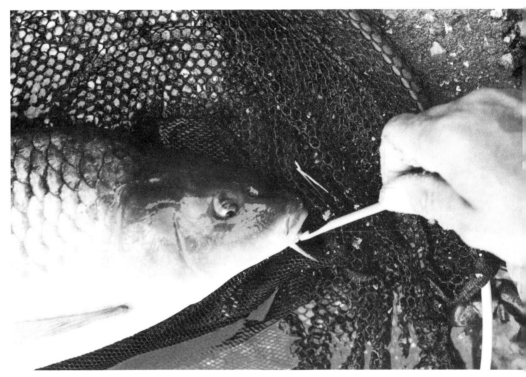

Use a disgorger or forceps to remove the hook unless it is on the lips, when fingers are equally as good.

Use a big landing net, and hold it by the meshes. Do not drag the fish across the bankside.

SLIDE *your fish into the net, don't* THROW.
And be sure the net is staked out in adequately deep water.

will prove invaluable. These can be used for removing hooks from both inside and outside the mouth.

Pike are the problem fish as far as handling is concerned. Anglers are scared of big pike and fail to master the muscle bound fish from the outset. A pike's mouth does look fearsome but providing you handle it correctly, dentistry is quite simple.

For unhooking pike you need several pieces of specialist equipment. A good strong leather glove is most useful – the gardener's type are best. An extra long pair of forceps is also a must. A strong pair of long nose pliers and a John Roberts treble hook remover could also prove useful if the hooks are firmly lodged.

Once the pike is in the landing net, leave

it there. Spread back the mesh to reveal the pike and then straddle it with the fish either lying on its side or back. With a gloved left hand ease open the lower jaw and remove the hooks with forceps. If the fish has taken the bait well down and its throat is hooked, you can either apply the long nosed forceps to free the steel, or use the Gardner treble hook remover. This is a long rod with a slotted end, and above the slot is a mushroom like shield. The rod is attached to the trace wire and pushed down on to the offending hook. Then with the wire kept taut push down and free the offending barb, twist and withdraw. The shield masks the three barbs on the hook as it is removed.

If the pike proves really difficult it is possible to carefully lift the gill cover plate and pass the nose of the forceps between the delicate rakers to the lodged hook. Care must be taken not to damage the rakers.

Once unhooked, fish can be retained in a variety of ways although it's probably best to return all fish once unhooked and admired. Small fish can be kept in minnow or micromesh keepnets. But make sure you use a large one staked out in plenty of water. Never lay a keepnet in shallow water, especially in summer.

Carp are best returned immediately, as are pike. However, for short periods it is possible to use a keepsack, a large black nylon bag with a drawstring at the top. Make sure the one you use has plenty of holes punched in the sides to allow air and water to pass through. Sacks, like keepnets, shouldn't be set out in shallow water. Try to find a deep hole, preferably in the shade. On second thoughts . . . why not leave your keepnet or sacks at home and take a camera instead! Cameras don't lie and are a lot kinder to the fish.

Other fishing books published by The Crowood Press

(A complete list of Crowood fishing books can be supplied upon request. Please write to the publishers at the address below.)

Rods & Rod Building *by Len Head, with illustrations by John Holden*

A manual of rod building which also offers in-depth guidance on the design and selection of rods for all major branches of fresh and saltwater fishing.
Illustrated with b&w and colour photographs and diagrams.
96 pages. 235 × 165mm. Hardback. £6.95.

An Introduction to Reservoir Trout Fishing *by Alan Pearson*

Tackle, casting, flies, bank and boat fishing and places to fish are a few of the topics covered in this useful beginner's guide.
Illustrated with b&w and colour photographs and diagrams.
136 pages. 210 × 130mm. Hardback. £5.95.

Long Distance Casting *by John Holden*

A guide to the tackle and techniques of long-range casting in saltwater.
Illustrated with b&w photographs and diagrams.
96 pages. 297 × 210mm. Hardback. £8.95.

Imitations of the Trout's World *by Bob Church & Peter Gathercole*

This book describes advanced fly tying techniques not widely known and, with the use of superb colour photography, explores the link between the natural and the artificial. Later in the book, the authors take the reader on a 'guided tour' of major waters in the British Isles when they relate local methods and give practical tips based on experience. A book no serious fisherman can afford to miss.
Illustrated with colour and b&w photographs and diagrams.
176 pages. 270 × 210mm. Hardback. £12.50.

In Visible Waters *by John Bailey*

In this book, beautifully illustrated with colour and line drawings, the author reveals the deep insight he has gained into the lives of the coarse fish species during nearly 30 years of close observation.
Illustrated with colour and line drawings.
156 pages. 245 × 180mm. Hardback. £9.95.

Books listed above are available through booksellers, but, in case of difficulty, please write to:
The Crowood Press, Ramsbury, Wiltshire, SN8 2HE, England.

The details listed above are correct at the time of going to press but are subject to alteration without prior notice.